1HQ
One Hard Question

Mark Artus

with Stephen Foster

One Hard Question

1HQ Limited,
The Old Brewery, 22 Russell Street, Windsor,
Berkshire SL4 1HQ, United Kingdom

t: +44 (0) 1753 624242

e: onehardquestion@1hq.co.uk

w: www.1hq.co.uk

All rights reserved. No part of this publication may be reproduced, stored in a retrieval system, or transmitted in any form by any means, electronic, mechanical, photocopying, recording or otherwise, without the prior permission of the copyright owners.

Edition 2/2011

© 1HQ Limited 2011

Contents

Preface		7
Introduction		9
1	One Hard Question	13
2	In the Beginning	27
3	The Times They Are a-Changin'	39
4	Even Further into the Beginning	51
5	Pile It High or Just Sell It?	61
6	Beauty That's More Than Skin Deep	73
7	The Medium Is the Message	85
8	The Consumer Is Not a Moron, She's Your Wife	97
9	And So To (More) Politics	109
10	And Then Came the Internet	123
11	Creatively Intelligent or Intelligently Creative?	137
12	There Are More Questions than Answers	149
Index		153

One Hard Question

To my patient & supportive family
Lucy, Ben, Charlie & Oliver

Preface

This book is an attempt to explain how great brands came into being and how companies and individuals can produce great brands today.

Our premise is that all these successes involved asking One Hard Question. The only way to find the right answer was to ask the right question in the first place. Of course, not all the examples discussed in the book are successes, but there's much to be learned from these too.

I hope you find the book interesting and useful whether you're a marketing executive, an agency person (of whatever ilk) or a student. Or just someone who'd like to understand a bit more about the brand-centric universe we live in.

I'd like to thank all the people who helped with the book, including Stephen Foster of The Editorial Partnership, David O'Reilly of The Editorial Partnership (who also contributed some of the text), Monica Allen for help with the final version, and my 1HQ team with their sharp brains (and pencils).

Mark Artus
Chief Executive
1HQ

Introduction

Einstein is quoted as having said that if he had one hour to save the world he would spend fifty-five minutes defining the problem and only five minutes finding the solution.

There is no doubt that we are in uncharted waters as a result of the seismic changes that have happened to our society over the past few years. The result being that we now struggle to trust anything and anyone. The bedrock of society has been based on the assumption that you need to be able to trust people, but there is no question that trust is sadly lacking in today's world.

For this very reason we need to turn back the clock and look hard at what we all do, why we do it and for what purpose, and explore the one hard question that will help to find the answers.

This book attempts to look at the hard questions throughout our business history that nobody wanted to ask or hoped they would not have to ask as the consequences were simply too difficult to comprehend or easy to contemplate. But throughout history some true pioneers did ask the hard questions and were not afraid of the outcome, as difficult as it may have been. Others failed to ask the right question because of arrogance or simply through stupidity.

Historians now dispute that Singapore could have been defended successfully from the invading Japanese in 1942 if some of the fortress's powerful guns had faced inland. The ill-prepared British would have lost the battle anyway, they say. But it's surely beyond doubt that more emphasis on the potential threat from the land as opposed to the sea would have greatly assisted the defenders. What do we do if we're attacked from the land, was a hard question that should surely have been posed, or, if it was, someone should have posed it more strongly.

Moving on to business, the decision in October 2009 to let Wall Street investment bank Lehman Brothers go to the wall brought the global financial system to the brink of collapse, in the process leading to the almost instant nationalisation of Lloyds Bank and Royal Bank of Scotland in the UK.

The then US Treasury Secretary Hank Paulson and his aides no doubt asked themselves what would happen if Lehman was allowed to fail but came up with the wrong answer, that the system could ride it out. In the end it did, of course, but not until billions of dollars had been spent and tens of thousands of people had lost their jobs in a savage global recession. The politicians and financial experts failed to take full account of the fact that Lehman was involved in millions of trades that affected most of the world's biggest banks and that interbank lending would shrivel until these trades were unravelled.

But we don't always get it wrong in business, as in other spheres, and this book explores the implications of some of the decisions that changed the course of business history.

Our particular subject is the world of branding and brand promotion, everything from advertising to design. The interesting element in all of this is not just the outcome but also the sequence of events that led to one hard question needing to be asked… and answered.

And here it's worth underlining that brands are not just commercial entities. The world's great religions are highly successful brands too. Political parties try their damnedest to be compelling brands.

Hard questions come in a variety of guises. Some are hard in the sense that it's just difficult to find the answer. What's the square root of 28? But the real hard questions are the ones that no one wants to ask or hopes they won't have to.

Arguably this is where creativity plays its most important role in business: identifying and asking the hard question that can

Introduction

then be turned into a creative solution. This process is not always easy from the outset, but the gap between strategy and creative execution has never been more important, as this is often where the magic happens.

We at 1HQ are not historians, or scholars for that matter, but we are inquisitive and we are restless, and we are interested in and passionate about finding the right questions, the ones that will lead to ground-breaking solutions.

The old adage that 'change is the only constant' is one thing that we can all be certain about, but the change that we will see as we climb out of this recession in our industry is going to be seismic and will lead to a different way of thinking.

It will also lead to new types of agencies, and we believe that 1HQ will be one of them.

1

One Hard Question

Important decisions about brands and markets are being taken all over the world, every minute, by a myriad of individuals and companies.

This may be to solve problems, help a company grow or just carry on doing what they do (companies these days feel they're not allowed to stand still).

Usually such processes are the result of collaboration between the client, the manufacturer or service supplier, and an agency of some kind. For years the lead agency was usually an advertising agency because advertising was seen as the key to brand growth.

There were exceptions, of course – inventors like James Dyson, with his cleaning machines, and Trevor Bayliss, the inventor of the wind-up radio. Or the various Silicon Valley wizards who saw the potential of computers and the internet before anyone else.

In the conventional commercial sector these brilliant people had their equivalents too: product design companies and new product development companies (the latter usually take in hand a product that's already been invented).

And what do these two groups have in common? That, at the right time, they have asked themselves One Hard Question about what they wanted to do or needed to do. And, when they found the answer, business as a whole, not just their business, took a quantum leap forward.

But what exactly constitutes a hard question? Well, 'what's the square root of 28?' is a hard question but we know there's an answer to it. Trying to split the atom or discover the structure of DNA were pretty hard questions for anyone to ask, although answers were, eventually, forthcoming. But if all the hard questions that need to be asked in the world of branding were like these then there wouldn't be many of us left in the business.

The hard questions we're discussing are those capable of transforming a business activity, and that's usually by providing an original, hitherto unthought-of or unregarded answer.

Some people would see this in terms of 'left brain or right brain,' the notion that the left side of the brain is where rational, logical impulses lie whereas the right side provides intuition and insight – creativity, to use another word. Whether or not this is good science, it's useful for our purposes. By and large it's possible to summarise client-side thinking as left brain, logical and, where possible, evidence-based, and agency thinking as right brain or creative.

Agencies are constantly frustrated by the habit of agency clients, the brand owners, to be reluctant to take any step that is not 'validated' by research. They know that when you ask people what they think they will usually refer to what they know already, hardly a good recipe for innovation.

Of course many clients are not necessarily looking to innovate, they are more concerned with growing the business incrementally or simply defending what they have achieved to date. The difficulty with this is that clients become trapped in their own tunnel vision; they just want to improve what they do already. In such circumstances it's rare for them to effect a quantitative leap in what they do. But it can happen.

Very often what pushes them that bit further is a touch of commercial desperation. Take Rupert Murdoch's BSkyB back in 1992. The company had been going for two years, after Sky Television had merged with satellite rival broadcaster British Satellite Broadcasting (after the Channel Tunnel, the UK's most expensive new business launch) and signed up a million subscribers to its pay-TV service. But it still seemed as far away as ever from making money; subscriptions

One Hard Question

didn't pay for the true cost of the technology and, in advertising terms, it was dwarfed by ITV and Channel 4.

ITV in the meantime had struck a deal to broadcast First Division football matches live on Sundays, a move the football authorities had resisted for decades as they thought it would harm gate receipts. This contract was coming up for renewal and most people thought there were two realistic bidders, ITV and the BBC, whose *Match of the Day* highlights show on Saturday was now looking rather old hat. Murdoch and his henchmen, Sam Chisholm and David Chance, faced an inescapable hard question. What can we do to make Sky pay? The alternative might have been the whole Murdoch empire landing in the hands of its bankers. They gambled that top-flight football would attract enough pay-TV punters to push the company into profit and also that ITV and the BBC would bid as low as they could because they would be confident that the football world would want its product on terrestrial TV with big audiences rather than the (mostly) unwatched Sky.

But the big football clubs were rather keen to get as much money as they could and they weren't at all concerned that most of the population wouldn't see their game on TV. This would, after all, support the gate receipts argument. So Sky somehow or other rustled up the money to bid far higher than ITV and the BBC, and what is now known as the Premier League, as opposed to the old First Division of the Football League, was formed.

Had ITV managed to find another few hundred million, which at the time it could easily afford, the whole development of football, not just in the UK but also across the world, might have been different. After all it was Sky's billions that inflated the price of football and footballers. In the four years to 1992 ITV had paid just £44 million for the football rights. Sky invested £304 million in its winning deal for the following five seasons and £670 million for the four years from 1997. It was a quantum leap into a new world for UK football and digital television. David Beckham made his Manchester United debut in 1992, the first year of the Sky deal and the Premier League. Without it he would almost certainly not be as rich and famous as he is now.

Sky's solution to its own hard question can be seen as a winning combination of left brain and right brain. The rational left told it that it had to increase subscribers, and therefore revenue, or die. The right side said let's change the world if we have to, even if that makes us the most unpopular company in the UK as we deprive all the free-to-air viewers of their football.

Through this synthesis of different types of thinking, Sky saw the big picture through a different lens and provided a tangible benefit that differentiated it from its rivals, a key requirement in successful branding. It perceived that consumers wanted more live football, the Premier League clubs were desperate for high revenues and Sky itself needed a guaranteed stream of loyal, committed subscribers. The deal was perfect for all parties.

The football coup was what today we might call a 'killer app'. By 1997 90 per cent of Sky subscribers were opting for its sports offering and 25 of its top 30 programmes were Premier League matches. Sky is now the richest and most powerful broadcaster in the UK and, in its various guises, across the world.

Often using the right side of the brain involves seeing the market in a totally different way, like turning a picture on its side or re-arranging a jigsaw. The marketplace may seem ossified, with no opportunities for a breakthrough, or it can look like a maze, a series of dead ends with no obvious way out.

Sometimes, making the breakthrough requires turning received wisdom on its head, thinking the impossible because there are no other ideas left. Take the invention of the Swatch, the response of the Swiss watchmaking industry to the Japanese quartz watches that were threatening to take over the industry in the 1970s. For decades the Swiss watch had been the gold standard of timekeeping. Filled with beautiful precision engineering made in a painstaking traditional manner, the Swiss mechanical movement watch was both the highest form of quality craftsmanship and a classic heritage product. More than a simple watch, it would be handed down from generation to generation and it symbolised historical continuity, family bonds and high status.

Before the 1970s the Swiss industry's dominance was such that it accounted for 30 per cent of the world's watch market, with a much higher share of the luxury end. Then came the Japanese and their quartz products. Within less than a decade the Swiss share had fallen to 9 per cent and was still dropping.

The Swiss watchmakers were facing extinction. They were losing out even in their traditional stronghold of high-quality timepieces. The writing was on the wall. Yet instead of retreating into their traditional conservatism or diluting or trying to jazz up their core product, the Swiss recognised that the world had changed and, faced with their own hard question, identified the answer: develop a brand with precisely the opposite characteristics and values to their traditional products. The Swatch was not built to last for generations but to be thrown away and replaced. It was made by robots, not craftsmen and was sealed into plastic cases so that it couldn't be repaired. It had 51 moving parts as opposed to the 125 of a typical mechanical watch. Most importantly, the Swatch was a fun, stylish fashion object, not a serious classic to be revered and handed down over time.

Developed by a consortium of Swiss manufacturers, manufacturing costs were kept low and so too were the prices. Consumers were invited to throw away their old Swatch and buy another. New colours and designs, which at first changed every six months and then more frequently, kept the market continuously stimulated and ready for more products. The brand's slogan was 'Always new, always different.' Within 15 years 200 million Swatches had been sold and the Swiss market share had soared to 50 per cent.

Swatch kept the necessary energy and impetus behind the brand with continuous line extensions and brand innovation. In addition to the standard plastic product, it brought out the Chrono and the Irony, while other novelties included the light-powered Swatch Solar, the MusiCall with a melodic alarm and the Beep Swatch, the world's first watch with a built-in pager.

The Swatch was a triumph of right-brain thinking, a brightly coloured, disposable watch that was the antithesis of all that Swiss watchmaking represented. And even more remarkable given that it was produced by a consortium. By throwing the traditional ideals, values and heritage that had served them so well up in the air the Swiss demonstrated how to look at a market completely afresh and then think freely to come up with something new that matched the way that consumers were starting to think and feel.

Other brands besides Sky are capable of applying right-brain thinking in some areas of their operation and left-brain thinking in others. Not always with completely successful results, however. From its early beginnings Apple exemplified the 'Chic, not geek' slogan that it later used for the launch of its iMac. In a market where PC commands were written in computerese and the machines all came in boring beige, Apple stood out for the simplicity and elegance of its operating system, the easily recognisable icons and the general user-friendliness of its whole brand.

Apple understood that computers had to be accessible to ordinary people and that design mattered. It viewed its products and operating systems in aesthetic terms and felt from the start that a computer could be a thing of beauty in the same way as a well-made piece of furniture. That was its right brain talking and that was how it connected to the consumer and for a while managed to corner a 20 per cent market share.

Unfortunately, when it came to doing business its left brain took over and refused to license its operating system to other computer manufacturers. Here Apple couldn't see the big picture and it handicapped itself severely, probably throwing away the chance for world dominance, because it was too rigid and wanted to keep too much control for itself. That left the door open for Bill Gates and the Microsoft MS-DOS system, which swept up the rest of the market. Apple went on to greater things but only after suffering severe problems. Once Steve Jobs, the company's founder who had been dumped disastrously by the Apple board, returned, the iMac, iPod, iPhone and iPad have maintained and built on its unique position as an iconoclastic, innovative, stylish brand, but it is still a niche company. It could all have been so different.

Juggling the left brain and right brain is far better than using no brain at all of course, as Coca-Cola found when it introduced 'new' Coke in 1985. The product was never officially named New Coke but that's how people reacted to it when Coca-Cola changed its celebrated secret formula to try to fend off competition from deadly rival Pepsi.

In research, consumers said they liked the new taste and, at first, the relaunch of arguably the world's biggest brand went fairly well, even though the company rather messed things up at the official launch event when it was unable to describe accurately what the new taste was and how it differed from the original. But Coke is a strange business, in that it depends on the activities of a large number of independent bottlers scattered over the globe; the Atlanta-based company produces the syrup and provides the marketing. And the bottlers were not best pleased at the change, neither were consumers in Coke's heartland of the US Deep South. Here Coke was regarded as part of the fabric of life precisely because of people's perception that it was just the same as it always had been. Or had been since 1935 when the formulation was changed to make it vegetarian and also suitable for kosher and halal tastes.

An almighty storm brewed up and so-called Classic Coke, the original formula, was re-introduced just 77 days after 'new' Coke's launch. New Coke was still sold for several years, proving popular with the denizens of Los Angeles on the West Coast but Classic Coke rapidly regained top spot in the market and eventually became just Coke. So Coca-Cola was quite literally back to square one after a great deal of fuss and corporate trauma.

'If it ain't broke don't fix it,' is one of those aphorisms it's hard to argue with, although it can be, of course, an excuse for lassitude and inertia. Coca-Cola itself has claimed that the New Coke farrago was actually a good thing because it re-energised the company. It also prompted it to reduce the number of its bottlers and tighten its control over them. And the company hit back strongly not just with Classic Coke but the launch of Cherry Coke, the favourite tipple of its long-term investor, the legendary Warren Buffett of investment company Berkshire Hathaway.

But recognising that consumers can't be led by the nose, however illogical their preferences may be, is a lesson that all companies have to learn and relearn from time to time. And it's indisputable that branding and promotion works best when it flatters the consumer and congratulates them on their fine taste in buying the brand.

This is clearly and obviously the case with luxury and big ticket items, but less obvious often on the supermarket shelves.

A recent subtle change to another iconic brand, Heinz Tomato Ketchup, testifies that it can be done. Heinz wished to remind consumers that tomatoes are good for you, particularly so in such a highly concentrated form. But bottled sauces and condiments are not immediate examples of healthy products; think of the numerous bottled pasta sauces that are regularly found to contain high levels of salt. Heinz's start point was 'tomato performance', a concept that describes accurately the merits of the fruit but is not especially appetising. This was deftly tweaked, at my company 1HQ actually, to 'grown, not made', an equally accurate description of how Heinz Tomato Ketchup is actually produced without additives, unlike some of its cheaper competitors. And is much more appetising.

These days, big companies also have to be mindful of the way their corporate behaviour can impact their brands. It becomes particularly pressing when, as they often do, they take over their smaller competitors or buy stakes in other companies.

Big brand owners, as we said, are far more left brain than right. They have systems and procedures from which only the bravest executive will dare to depart, and they rely on their marketing communications agencies to provide the clever, right-brain stuff. And very often ignore their expensive advice. But successful new businesses are usually a triumph of right brain over left. The people who set them up, entrepreneurs, are prepared to back their own intuition with their own money and, accordingly, quite often lose it all. But some succeed.

But big companies value these smaller businesses as much for the creative ingenuity that has gone into them as for the contribution they hope they will make to the financial bottom line. And the entrepreneurs, usually, are prepared to take the big company bucks eventually. Not just for the obvious reason but also because, in most markets, keeping the company growing means putting in ever-greater investment. Rolling the financial dice too many times might mean that they risk losing the gains they have invested so much time and money in.

In the food sector big companies can help their smaller brethren fight their corner with the supermarkets so they are listed on reasonable terms, increase production and expand internationally. The trouble is that a lot of customers don't like this very much.

In the UK Innocent, the smoothies drinks company, sold a 58 per cent stake to Coca-Cola for all of the above reasons. But many long-time Innocent supporters do not find the association with the ultimate heavily marketed, mass-produced and overly packaged soft drink at all appealing. In 2005 fair trade and organic chocolate maker Green & Black's sold out to Cadbury for a rather modest £20 million and back in 2000 US ice cream maker Ben and Jerry's, the ultimate hippy business, shocked its supporters by selling to Unilever.

In 2001 UK sandwich chain Pret A Manger, which markets itself on its fresh and natural ingredients, although some might argue with

One Hard Question

that, sold a stake to burger giant McDonald's whose products at the time (although they have since changed somewhat) were nobody's idea of fresh and natural. Pret didn't start selling McDonald's burgers, even in America where McDonald's tried to help it expand, but the association didn't help either party. McDonald's sold back its stake but this meant Pret selling all of itself to investors headed by venture capital firm Bridgepoint and mighty investment bank Goldman Sachs.

Are the above brands tarnished by their financial arrangements with much bigger and, to many people, far less appealing companies? Arguably they are to a certain extent.

Does the big company ownership or association mean that they too have becoming boring, procedure-driven left-brain companies? It's probably too early to say, although one can't imagine a Unilever-owned Ben and Jerry's launching a new product, Cherry Garcia, to honour the founders' favourite musician, the late Jerry Garcia of the Grateful Dead.

In many of the examples in this book, companies have found themselves confronted by brand boundaries imposed on them internally – by the limits of their own traditions, skills processes or technologies – or by external constraints in the marketplace. And of course they have sometimes broken through these boundaries very successfully.

Yet there are some companies which seem never to have acknowledged the possibility of boundaries or obstacles which could not be overcome. Yamaha, the Japanese company now 120 years old, is one such.

Since the 1950s it has managed to extend its brand from musical instruments to motorbikes and even to bathtubs, as if this were the most natural thing in the world. Founded in 1887 by Torakusu Yamaha, the company started off making pianos and organs and won several prizes at the St Louis World Fair in 1904. Fast forward to the 1950s when the then president Genichi Kawakami was looking for

One Hard Question

a way to keep some old production machinery in use and thought 125cc motorbikes were the answer. It took some years of design and equipment modification but then the first model rolled off the line. From there Yamaha moved into motorcars, archery equipment and skis. It kept to its musical heritage with trumpets, guitars and drumkits but then brought out the bathtub. The company has continued to view the marketplace in a different way from most other large groups. Tennis racquets, golf clubs, ski boots and industrial robots have followed from its production lines.

Rather like the days when every business put the owner's name above the door, Yamaha simply asks the consumer to trust in its name and reputation. It has enough confidence in its design, engineering and commitment to quality to engage in what for most other companies would seem crazy product diversification. And it has been successful in just about every market it has entered. Consumers buy Yamaha products confident that the name means quality.

But the great enabler in modern business is, of course, the internet and sometimes, in a wonderful fusion of left and right brain, it allows people to do something they've dreamed of for decades, even centuries.

Take betting.

The extremely hard question punters have been asking themselves for all this time is, 'How do I beat the bookmakers?' Bookies set the odds, chose which bets they would take and even which clients they would accept (ones who didn't win too often) and never had to worry much about competition outside their circle because for years you had to have a government licence to be a bookmaker.

And the authorities, in the US and UK, came down hard on 'illegal' bookmakers, even freelance individuals, because such activities were regarded as a front for gangsterism and the perfect way for criminals to launder stolen money. The big bookies in the UK prospered mightily in this comfortable universe, losing regularly to only a small band of very clever (or lucky) punters who would sooner or later find that their accounts were closed. With their betting shop networks and the expansion into telephone betting, there were no real clouds on the horizon. Then came the internet, and some of them were quick to set up internet betting services too, even moving 'offshore' for tax purposes, with Gibraltar proving to be a highly accommodating address.

But in 2000 two young entrepreneurs, Andrew Black and Edward Wray, realised this was also the way to give the punters what they wanted, by changing the question or rather the proposition. It was no longer 'How do I beat the bookie?' but 'You be the bookie yourself'.

Betfair was, and is, an internet betting exchange which for the first time allowed punters (as opposed to only bookmakers) to lay bets on horses to lose as well as win. Now quite clearly in any given race more horses lose than win and previously these nags had been a steady revenue stream for the bookies only. Now anyone could back their judgement in the market if they were brave enough to do so. Betfair, now the world's biggest internet betting exchange with around two million customers, makes its money on a 5 per cent level on winnings (less for some big punters) which, with turnover of around £50 million a week is a substantial sum. The bookies, of course, are still outraged, claiming that Betfair is open to corrupt parties who nobble horses, although this has been going on as long as horse racing itself. Betfair punters also have the advantage over bookies in that they don't have to offer odds on every horse in the race. The business has expanded internationally despite fierce opposition from the bookmaking fraternity and some legislators, apart from in the US, where internet gambling of any sort is banned. Internet gambling executives from the UK have even been clapped in irons in the US as they got off the plane.

The internet has also revolutionised other forms of gambling, most notably poker, with, for the first time, people able to play for small stakes without the hassle of visiting a licensed casino (which probably wouldn't accept small stakes anyway). One can argue all day about the ethics of gambling, on the internet or elsewhere. But the case of Betfair, at least, points to the ability of entrepreneurs to bring about radical change by providing a truly original solution to an age-old question.

Not every solution to a problem is so radical but even seemingly small changes to a brand can cost millions and lead to far-reaching consequences, for better or worse. And every day the stakes are being raised as business becomes more centralised and global. Unlike our friends at Yamaha, most companies like to stick to their last, make similar products and present them to consumers in the same way.

This is partly because of supposed economies of scale. These can be deceptive in the extreme, and never more so than in the world of advertising, marketing and promotion. Many global marketing directors and agency account directors spend their life in a fruitless quest for the campaign that works as well in China and Slovenia as it does in the US, UK, France or Germany. The facts of the matter are that, with a few exceptions such as luxury goods and maybe cars and entertainment, the way consumers perceive and value these brands and the way they respond to marketing communications vary wildly.

Brand names can be a particular bugbear. There used to be a famous French soft drink called Pschitt, owned by Perrier. The name replicated the sound when the bottle was opened, which was fair enough. Unlike, say, its French rival Orangina, Pschitt failed to fly with Anglo-Saxon consumers for obvious reasons and therefore never became an international brand.

In advertising, the British famously enjoy humour and a self-deprecating tone of voice that some American companies and consumers still struggle with. Selling remains a serious business in the US and arguably it's becoming more serious elsewhere in the world too. The French will cheerfully introduce sexual imagery into anything, as indeed most creatives anywhere will, given half a chance. The Germans are supposed to lack a sense of humour entirely, although this is doubtless an exaggeration.

And some might say that these are national stereotypes that we can do without, but advertising, like all marketing communications, is a form of shorthand and so are such stereotypes.

It's hard enough to devise and implement marketing improvements in just one market, let alone across the world. But that's the challenge facing brand owners and their agencies today. That one hard question (if you need to ask more than one you're probably barking up the wrong tree) just got much harder.

2

In the Beginning

Success has many fathers, or so they say, while failure is an orphan.

And when we look at successful brands – from Coca-Cola to Dove soap to Goldman Sachs – common sense tells us that there must be a multitude of reasons why they have succeeded.

But I'm going to suggest that in each case the people who created the brand asked themselves 'one hard question' and that, when they found the answer, that decision played the major part in creating most of today's huge brands and, in many cases, whole companies.

For many years the word 'brand' was synonymous with 'product', just a cooler title. 'What brand do you smoke?' they used to say in cigarette commercials in those far-off days when they were allowed.

But brand has come to mean something else, a magical kind of super-product that floats about in the commercial ether, guaranteeing sales and profits despite the frantic efforts of competitors and the eternal vicissitudes of business life.

To add to the confusion, these other products call themselves brands too.

A strong brand can overcome all sorts of hurdles, from calamitous product failure (although Perrier mineral water didn't) to stupendous marketing cock-ups because of its so-called brand equity and the trust and value it has built up over many years of satisfying customers (or successfully persuading them that they're satisfied).

This, we are told, is why the famous American investor Warren Buffett, chairman of the Berkshire Hathaway investment company is so rich. He invested in Coca-Cola back in the 1950s, in due course became a director and was still on the board in 2009, staying loyal to

One Hard Question

the company through the self-inflicted disaster of mucking around with the brand with the calamitous launch of 'new' Coke. Warren himself drinks mainly Cherry Coke at his Omaha headquarters.

And he's also a big investor in Kraft, another of the giant American consumer product companies, which markets famous brands such as Oreo biscuits and Dairylea processed cheese slices. Kraft, of course, bought the famous British confectionery company Cadbury, despite Buffet's opposition (he thought it paid too much). Buffett also bought a huge tranche of shares in investment bank Goldman Sachs in the fall of 2008 when even that famous institution was wobbling precipitately in the wake of the Lehman Brothers collapse. Goldman, in its own way, is just as much a brand as Oreo.

But, you may say, all products are called 'brands' these days, however useless or unoriginal they may be. Even what used to be called supermarket 'own label' products are called 'own brands'. So why do they matter and how can we tell one that works from all the ones that don't?

We could call the ones we're discussing 'superbrands' but that's been done before and, in any case, successful brands don't have to be mega-products. Quirky British products like Stain Devils and Fisherman's Friend cough sweets are successful brands.

In the best of all possible worlds a brand's worth can be computed by the profit it makes for its lucky owner, but that's not always the case by any means. Arguably the most famous brand in the newspaper market is *The Times* but that particular London newspaper hasn't made money since, well, ever, maybe. But that didn't stop supposedly hard-nosed newspaper publisher Rupert Murdoch buying it in 1985 and sticking with it ever since, even though it's estimated to have cost him many millions, consistently, in the intervening period.

Did he ever suppose it would make a profit? Shortly after buying it he launched a price-cutting campaign against his main rival, the then profitable *Daily Telegraph*. His thinking may have been that, if the *Telegraph* were to be taken out of the market or seriously enfeebled, then *The Times* would sweep up its readers and advertisers and become profitable. But the *Telegraph* hung on, despite the ministrations of subsequently imprisoned owner Conrad Black, and is still responsible for more black ink in the profit and loss account than *The Times* is. So is it just a 'trophy' brand? It's worth something to someone because it's famous? Murdoch is clearly determined to get better value from *The Times*, hence his establishment of the controversial paywall for online readers of the newspapers in his stable. Whether this will help to turn *The Times* into a paying proposition remains to be seen.

Trophy brands are hardly unique to the newspaper business of course, nor to other industries such as fashion, retailing and high-end cars.

One dictionary definition of brand is an iron stamp for burning a mark; another is something that shows ownership or quality. A third suggestion is something that impresses itself on the memory. The brands we are to discuss here have aspects of all three; they are superior, or at least adequate, products which enjoy a strong identity in a crowded world and so linger in the memory (and find their way onto the shopping lists) of millions of consumers.

That doesn't guarantee they'll make money, of course, but the possession of one or more of these attributes should be a hell of a good start. And it helps too if the brand owner knows how to maximise the value of their brand. To do this the company needs to know what the brand offers and what makes this compelling (assuming it is, of course).

The brand owner needs, above all, to determine what is the single, distinctive, motivating truth about the brand in question – what makes it special and attractive? Of all the hard questions to ask, this is the most enduring. This will change over time as the world and consumer preferences change. But many famous brands, and companies, manage to change in tandem.

To try to find out why these brands and companies have succeeded let's look first at a business practice or process; the bit of architecture

One Hard Question

that made modern brands possible.

We begin our investigation in the town of Cincinnati, Ohio. The year is 1837 and an important conversation is taking place between one Alexander Norris and his newly acquired sons-in-law. In a different era one of the world's biggest and most famous companies might have been called Norris & Norris, had Alexander entrusted his scheme to his daughters. But 1837 was a man's world and Alexander managed to persuade his sons-in-law, William Procter, a candlemaker, and James Gamble, a soapmaker, to form Procter & Gamble.

Like many successful companies P&G had a good war in its history, in this case the American Civil War from 1861 to 1865, when it was contracted to supply the victorious Union army with, yes you've guessed it, candles and soap. When peace came, P&G had many thousands of presumably satisfied customers on its hands, turning what was already a substantial business (its sales had reached the magic million dollars in 1859) into one of the nascent giants of the capitalist world. A further breakthrough came in the 1880s when it launched a new, inexpensive soap (soaps were then still regarded by many as luxuries) called Ivory. The big thing about Ivory was that it floated in water, so you didn't have to fumble around at the bottom of the bath. At the time this was a big product benefit, a theme that was going to play an important part in the life of P&G.

The company got bigger and bigger with more and more products. Among other things it pioneered the use of media promotion, sponsoring radio shows in the US from the 1920s onwards – 'soap operas'. But size and an ever-expanding product range can bring problems too and they became apparent to a young man called Neil Hosler McElroy, a Harvard graduate who joined the company's advertising department in 1925 (he was later to become president of the company and then US President Dwight D Eisenhower's defence secretary). McElroy became frustrated when working on Camay soap, because he found he was competing with P&G's venerable

In the Beginning

Ivory just as much as with offerings from rivals Lever Brothers and Palmolive. He realised the company needed to find a way to market Camay without affecting, or 'cannibalising', its other brands; a way of aiming it at a different group of consumers who wouldn't buy it instead of the famous floating Ivory.

This was the one hard question McElroy asked himself and the solution to it changed the world of marketing and 'brands' fundamentally.

His answer was contained in a famous memo to the directors in which he suggested that Camay receive more dedicated attention with, instead of one person in charge of it, a whole team in place. These people would 'run' Camay as if it was a separate business, seeking out new markets and being responsible for the brand's profit and loss. Thus was born the theory of brand management, where most brand decisions are decentralised to a dedicated group reporting eventually to a central board.

Its rapid adoption by P&G and then by other similar companies such as Unilever, Colgate-Palmolive, Kraft and General Foods (known in the trade as fast-moving consumer goods or FMCG companies) ushered in the era of modern marketing and brands as we know them today. It enabled these companies to market scores of brands in lots of different sectors, the only similarity often being that they were (relatively) low-priced, everyday items. Today P&G markets everything from Ariel washing powder to Pringles snacks.

But the McElroy memo led to more than just a group of companies who were successful at selling their brands in what we now call supermarkets. It helped to create the modern American way of doing business, one that has more or less conquered the economic world and also affected the way we think about nearly everything from political parties and government institutions to charities and our own personal health and well-being.

Like it or not, pretty much everything is seen as a brand these days, however appropriate or not that may be. And most companies

One Hard Question

and organisations now have people called, or who correspond to, in ascending order, product managers (the lowest form of marketing life), brand managers, marketing managers and marketing directors. These days the marketing director is increasingly termed the 'chief marketing officer' (as in chief executive officer) but never mind.

Anyway, back to P&G. Suitably armed with its new divisions of shock troops (the brand management teams) P&G set out to rule the world. But it didn't just need a structure, it needed better products (or so it assumed): soaps like Ivory which floated on top of the water or Camay which produced more foamy bits than all those other medical-sounding ones that people used to scrub themselves with.

This was another hard question P&G marketing folk asked themselves, as they searched for the distinctive, motivating truth; what makes this product better than the competition? And it required such product attributes for all its brands, sometimes with revolutionary effect.

P&G launched Pampers disposable diapers in 1961, thus releasing millions of women from the daily, if not hourly, chore of washing and trying to dry cloth nappies. In the 1960s, outside the US at least, most women didn't have washing machines or spin dryers so this was an onerous chore. Other companies, including healthcare giant Johnson & Johnson, were aware of the problem (you could hardly fail to be) but their products had failed to take off. But the brand wizards from Cincinnati were experts at selling product benefits persuasively and the world began to change.

So where did it all go wrong?

Well for P&G it didn't. In 2008 the company was the 8th largest in the world by market capitalisation and the 14th by profit, although its profits have flattened somewhat since. It has acquired a number of companies in different sectors which, for the most part, it has absorbed seamlessly and successfully. These include Richardson-Vicks in 1985 (when it acquired Oil of Olay), Clairol in 2001, Wella in

In the Beginning

2003 and the biggest, $57 billion Gillette, in 2005.

It is the biggest advertiser in the US (a subject to which we'll return), spending a staggering $2.62 billion in the US in 2008 although this figure has also fallen as advertisers generally have grappled with recession and a changing media landscape. But, in the greater scheme of things, Mr Norris's sons-in-law and their successors have done well.

Nonetheless, the company is seen as unduly mechanistic by some, its rigid adherence to the brand management structure and the pushing of clearly defined benefits in its advertising perhaps showing their age at last. Advertising is a particular *bête noire* with many former P&G staff and the company's advertising agencies. Although the company has tried to become more flexible recently, regularly sending troops of executives to the annual Cannes Golden Lions Awards that celebrate creativity in advertising worldwide, the company's ads are still built around the expression of a product benefit, often at the expense of wit and charm.

Typically they consist of two women chatting in a kitchen (the 'two Cs in a K' referred to by generations of bitter creative types), often accompanied by winsome children. This may have worked brilliantly in the 1950s and 60s when 'brands' which offered an alternative to household drudgery were seriously fascinating (as these new-fangled commercials were to many) but people today, most of us believe, aren't like that any more.

But the company has always believed that it knew what made consumers tick and history suggests it wasn't far wrong. And a few decades ago other influential voices thought so too.

One such was Rosser Reeves, a Madison Avenue advertising man who founded the Ted Bates advertising agency with his eponymous partner. Some pundits say that Don Draper, the slick creative director in the US TV series *Mad Men* is based on him. In the years after World War Two, advertising became a booming trade, chiefly by helping the likes of P&G and General Motors to

One Hard Question

sell their proposition to consumers in the US and then worldwide. The big agencies were divided into three groups of people, the first were called account men (advertising being mostly a male preserve in those days) who looked after the client and tried to ensure the second group, the creators or creatives, produced ads which more or less matched the client's brief and appeared on time. The third were media men who planned and bought the advertising time and space using the client's money. For this combination of services the agency extracted a generous commission from the advertiser, usually 15 per cent of the money spent in the media.

When press and magazines ruled the roost before the advent of commercial television, creatives were divided into copywriters and visualisers who would dream up the ads and then hand them over to the art studio to finish. When TV arrived visualisers cleverly rebranded themselves as art directors. The creative director sat on top of this motley crew. Creatives were often frustrated or 'resting' writers or artists. In the UK famous novelists Fay Weldon and Salman Rushdie once toiled at ad agency Ogilvy & Mather (Weldon was responsible for the famous slogan 'Go to work on an egg'). As such they kicked against discipline of any sort, particularly of the tablets of stone variety handed down by the likes of P&G. This clearly led to problems, although the creatives were to get their way, in some agencies and markets anyway, in the end.

Rosser Reeves, who was born in 1910, thought all this worryingly imprecise and rather a fraud on the client – it seemed just too hit and miss. Reeves wanted something that worked every time. Like many in advertising after him, he came up with his own hard question: 'How can advertising become more scientific?' His answer, inevitably reductionist, was that the only thing that mattered to the client was the sales figures; things like 'brand image' were for the birds.

To work, an ad had to show that the brand was superior to all its competitors, the P&G approach. But he went further in decreeing that any brand without such an advantage shouldn't be advertised until it had one; the advertising money would be better spent improving the product. But when it did reach this status the advantage — which he called the 'unique selling proposition' — should be forcibly and consistently expressed, often via a demonstration.

And once the USP had been ascertained, often summarised for the benefit of the consumer in a jingle such as 'melt in your mouth, not in your hand' for Mars' M&Ms, it should not be changed. UK readers with a long memory may recall this slogan being used for another Mars brand, Treets. They will certainly remember 'A Mars a day helps you work, rest and play'.

This motivating 'truth' would then be battered into consumers' brains by heavyweight barrages of TV advertising, orchestrated by the media men. So agencies might run essentially the same campaign for years but still enjoy their (at that time) 15 per cent commission on the media used. After all, why change it if it isn't broken? And the end result was a happy client because of the sales figures achieved and a happy agency because of the commission received.

Reeves set down his ideas in his 1961 book *Reality in Advertising* (he died in 1984). His ideas have not proved as enduring as P&G's brand management system because quite clearly not every product can have a *unique* selling proposition. You would end up with very few brands on the TV. It's sadly necessary to try to find some other way of differentiating them. Even P&G would reluctantly admit this. The Ted Bates agency, now absorbed into the French Publicis empire, profited mightily from the synergy between Reeves' thinking and P&G though, with P&G among its biggest accounts for decades.

There's another intriguing connection between Reeves and P&G's memo man Neil McElroy: President Eisenhower. McElroy, as we've mentioned, went on to be Eisenhower's defence secretary in 1957, to the surprise of many as selling soap and shampoo is not a particularly martial activity despite marketing adopting many military terms such as 'campaign' for its own purposes. As defence secretary, McElroy spent much of his time trying to close the so-called 'missile gap' between the US and the Soviet Union, which had stolen a march on the US in the mid-1950s. In this he was largely successful. So former Allied supreme commander Eisenhower had a high regard for these marketing men.

In 1952 war hero Eisenhower had been chosen by the Republican Party to contest the US presidency against Governor Adlai Stevenson II from Illinois, who was chosen by the Democrats when President Harry Truman decided not to run. He promptly enlisted the services of Reeves who produced a series of commercials featuring a split screen which showed Eisenhower apparently answering questions from voters in that avuncular way of his. In reality Reeves had just filmed Eisenhower talking and then crafted the questions to fit what he said.

At a pinch you might say that Eisenhower's war hero status was his USP. What was certain was that Reeves had helped to turn Eisenhower into a brand, arguably the first politician (although far from the last) to receive the brand management treatment. The downside to this was that political brands now had to take on the attributes of supermarket brands, be squeaky clean and inspire trust for a start. But Ike's chosen successor Richard Milhous Nixon (however hard he tried) was certainly not the epitome of the brand values Ike had been depicted so successfully as representing. Nixon, of course, lost narrowly to John Kennedy, a newer and far more potent brand (although political professionals will tell you that he won because his former bootlegger father Joe fixed the vote in Illinois).

But the point of this is that the hard question that P&G's Neil McElroy asked back in 1925 became a big part of the way Americans did business and this, in turn, fairly rapidly affected every part of American life.

In the meantime American brands had surged across the world with the speed of Attila the Hun and the seeming solidity of the Roman Empire. To a large degree they're still there. Coke and

In the Beginning

Pepsi still dominate in soft drinks, Kraft is the world's second-largest food company after Swiss-based Nestlé, P&G is the world's biggest consumer goods company (narrowly ahead of the Anglo-Dutch conglomerate Unilever) and the country dominates the global entertainment industry.

'Hollywood' itself is a classic brand. It may, in mundane physical reality, be a rather tacky sign on a Los Angeles hillside but it has come to stand for glitz, glamour, aspiration and dreams.

The US car industry – General Motors was until recently the second-largest advertiser after P&G – hasn't fared quite so well of course but that's because it chose to operate in a kind of time and space warp that ignored what was going on in the rest of the world. In this case the brand management storm troops and their advertising sidekicks got it spectacularly wrong.

So McElroy's memo has certainly earned its corn. But what happened next?

3

The Times They Are a-Changin'

Building global-beating brands in the 1950s and 60s was pretty straightforward by contemporary standards; taking the Procter & Gamble path you found a product advantage, expressed it clearly in a television campaign and spent bucket-loads of dollars persuading consumers to trial it.

If there was indeed a product advantage that people found useful, retailers would stock your product and consumers would buy it. And you were in a good position to fight off dreaded 'me too' products from your competitors.

Interestingly the corporate entity P&G has never tried to trade on its long record of supplying consumers with things they want; you won't see any reference to P&G in its consumer ads. Each brand has to make its own way, just as Neil McElroy intended. But that's enough P&G for now; how did the times, and the hard questions to be asked, change?

Bob Dylan released his famous song on his third album, of the same name, in 1964. For millions of people it summed up the fears, frustrations and aspirations of the decade of change that was the 1960s. Dylan himself, famously reluctant to provide any kind of explanation for his work, once remarked that it was (in part at least) a response to the American civil rights movement.

Anyway, the times certainly were a-changin' in the 1960s, although, for the majority of people, not quite in the way that Dylan and many others hoped. Yes, many young people were revolting in the US, UK and parts of Europe, sometimes in a political sense, more generally in terms of culture, music especially, and sexual mores. There was a revolution going on in the arts; in music obviously but also in the visual arts with Pop Art and the like and in related fields like fashion. Mary Quant's mini-skirts were regarded by some as rattling the foundations of society. The ultra-restrictive censorship of the 1950s and early 1960s more or less unravelled, although other restrictions were introduced, on so-called soft drugs, for example.

Most people were blissfully unaware of this until the end of the decade but, across what we used to call the developed world, consumers were definitely becoming more prosperous. They were now used to having a range of consumer choices; most people had a car of some sort, washing machines and fridges were the norm and the supermarket was becoming the core shopping experience, for food and household goods anyway. And brands were springing up like mushrooms on a rainy night.

This had already begun to attract its critics. Pundits would rail at what they called 'conspicuous consumption'. There was much discussion of what was called, disapprovingly of course, the 'consumer society'. There was a growing feeling in some quarters that companies, chiefly in their role as advertisers, were somehow conning us, persuading us to buy things we didn't need or that just weren't any good or positively harmful.

The event that crystallised this for many people was the publication of research that clearly demonstrated the link between smoking and lung cancer, and the dawning realisation that the tobacco industry had known about this link for years but striven with might and main to suppress it.

And this 'consumerist' movement, as it became, was also fuelled by a number of influential books, chiefly Vance Packard's *The Hidden Persuaders*, published in the US in 1957. Packard was a former magazine journalist and scientific populariser. Prior to *The Hidden Persuaders* his works included *How to Pick a Mate*, written in tandem with the Pennsylvania marriage counselling service, and *Animal IQ*.

The Hidden Persuaders concentrated on advertising and its use of

The Times They Are a-Changin'

what was called consumer motivational research, then greatly in vogue among advertising agencies in the Rosser Reeves era. Packard maintained that such uses of behavioural science in advertising were immoral as they were being used freely to brainwash us all into buying stuff we didn't really want. He went further and suggested that some advertisers were inserting subliminal messages in their commercials, unbeknown to us. A case of P&G meets *The Manchurian Candidate*. This was compelling stuff in a decade already fascinated by conspiracy theories but Packard had a point. We, the people, were being battered by almost wholly unfettered brand messages and some of the senders of these, like cigarette companies, were clearly up to no good.

But a wide choice of brands had become, for many people, the spice of life. It was certainly an important lubricant for many businesses and thus national economies, and not just in the US.

Take Scotland, which has a population roughly a hundredth of the size of the US, and its most famous product. A lot of people can't taste the difference between whisky and brandy in a blind taste test, let alone between a highland and an island malt or a single malt and a cheaper, blended whisky. But there are literally hundreds of Scottish whisky brands (reasonably enough as most originated from different distilleries and are, thus, different) including a large number of mostly mass-market blends. The blenders would say these are different too as the proportions of the grains they blend are different and water from different sources is used. But it's a fine point.

But people enjoy these many and varied brands, whether or not they can actually taste the difference between them. In the blended market drinks giant Diageo has for decades been happily selling a blend, Johnnie Walker Black Label, to affluent drinkers in the Far East at a price premium to make you blush. And that's what some brands can do and it certainly keeps the wheels of commerce in Scotland turning.

But how has our love affair with brands survived the criticisms of Packard and his followers?

One Hard Question

Well many brands, like whisky brands, can be described as lifestyle or aspirational choices. To a degree all brands can of course. Camay soap may be a mainstream supermarket brand but its ads used to feature a glamorous model soaping herself luxuriously amid a mountain of bubbles. So it was selling a treat as well as soap.

A famous old ad agency maxim, apropos sausages, is that you sell the sizzle (of the sausage in the pan, this was in the days when we used to fry everything) rather than the sausage (then mostly consisting of breadcrumbs, if not worse). But you need soap to wash and sausages, or something similar, to eat so there was a utility element to the purchase. And such products then, as now, can go a long way with simple product demonstrations in their ad campaigns.

But lots of brands, as Packard pointed out, you don't really need at all. And the one hard question marketers need to ask themselves about these is: 'How do we make this brand (which consumers don't actually need) compelling in the marketplace?'

Readers who were paying attention in the last chapter may say, by determining the distinctive, motivating truth about the brand. And that's true of course but in other sectors that motivating truth may well be based on the brand's communications rather than its nature as a physical product. The sizzle not the sausage.

Let's go back to Mr Dylan. In the 1960s the times were changing and people wanted more – more freedom, more rights and more, er, brands. And they were increasingly aware that they were being sold to, whether or not they'd read or even heard of Mr Packard. TV ads, for example, had become for many an annoying interruption to the programmes rather than a new and wonderful shop window on a world stuffed with goodies.

A small number were also aware of and heavily influenced by the cultural turmoil of the 1960s, from the new forms of artistic expression to the studied irreverence that was becoming the norm in comedy and film. And many of these people worked in the various companies that had sprung up to service the marketing community.

The Times They Are a-Changin'

These included advertising agencies, the kings of New York's famed Madison Avenue, design and public relations agencies, so-called sales promotions agencies which helped clients promote their products in store or on packs with money-off and 'free' gift promotions, photographers, art studios and the various film production companies who actually made the commercials.

Why, you might ask, were all these characters needed to help what were, in those days, big and quite lavishly staffed companies carry out a pretty important part of their business – selling their brands?

In part it was because most companies employed the P&G brand management system described in Chapter 2. If you empower a team of highly competitive people they will nearly always go out and spend the company's money on other people who they believe will improve the company's performance and in so doing further their own careers.

In part, in terms of advertising at least, it was because of history. Ad agencies had begun in the US in the 19th century, working for newspapers not advertisers. The newspapers had paid them commission to sell the ads, which is why agencies today are still often (not always) paid by commission on media expenditure.

This system then transmuted into one in which the agencies began producing ads for the client and bought the space too. It suited everybody for the agency, not the client, to be the financial principal in the transaction: the agency could subtract its commission from the money the client paid for the space while the system also ensured that the client paid up. If it didn't the ads didn't run.

The newspapers were happy for the agency to take its cut because it preferred to deal with a (relatively) small number of agencies, each handling a number of clients, rather than individual advertisers scattered across the length and breadth of America.

So ad agencies were there anyway. The third reason clients decided not to create their own ads and designs and, later on, funny stuff like PR was because they weren't very good at it.

The best creative talent preferred to work for agencies (of whatever kind) where they could work on a variety of clients rather than spending their life, as at one stage P&G's Neil McElroy did, just working on Camay. Agencies also tended to pay a lot more than clients and allow their favoured staff a more relaxed lifestyle, such as fancy cars, lots of trips and long, well-lubricated lunches – the famed Madison Avenue 'three martini' lunch.

The flip side of all this was that, if you lost the account, you might very well lose your job, account men even more so than creatives. This is the plot of Neil Simon's play *The Prisoner of Second Avenue*, which was filmed in 1974 with Jack Lemmon and Anne Bancroft. So life in the creative department tended to be a lively affair, with insecurity vying with master of the universe pretensions, much like Wall Street and the City of London today. But, in successful agencies, design as well as advertising, there were some rare talents and they were damned if they going to produce the same boring old ads or even, in some cases, what the client had asked for.

For aspirational brands, and these included everything from cars through booze and perfumes to cigarettes, this somewhat adversarial business environment produced some great hits and few big misses. And some terrific brands.

Few professionals would argue that Marlboro was, maybe is, a terrific brand. It cleverly appropriated the notion of 'Marlboro country', which was peopled with rugged cowboys who, later on in the campaign, didn't even need to be depicted puffing away on their favourite brand. A man on a horse with a few mountains in the distance came to symbolise Marlboro cigarettes, which is exactly what you want a brand to do. It was unfortunate that two of the 'cowboys' depicted in the campaign subsequently died of lung cancer, but there you go.

This 'trick', of the environment in the ads standing for the brand without actually needing to show the product, helped cigarette companies enormously as restrictions on tobacco promotion tightened. Cigarette marketers had always placed great store on the pack design; some of them like Camel or Player's Navy Cut, were mini-masterpieces in their own right. Once upon a time they used to have equally noteworthy cigarette cards in them of course, just the thing to appeal to under-age smokers. When restrictions tightened in the UK, Silk Cut, which had originally been sold on a low-tar platform as health fears affected the market, ran a striking series of posters taking the purple and white of the pack and turning them into white slashes on an imperial purple canvas. This was controversial in itself as some people thought they resembled knife slashes.

These ads were the work of the celebrated Charles Saatchi at his London mega-agency Saatchi & Saatchi. Saatchi, now better known as an art collector, had made his name as a copywriter at ad agency Collett Dickenson Pearce but, by the time these ads appeared in the 1970s and 80s, copywriters and art directors were more or less indistinguishable. Earlier in his career he had produced a celebrated 'anti-smoking' campaign for the Department of Health that showed the gunk smokers inflicted on themselves in gruesome detail. But, as he remarked recently, he himself had been puffing away happily as he did this.

One of CDP's tobacco clients was Benson & Hedges and it was famous for its gold pack. When it was no longer allowed to talk about the product it ran posters and a celebrated cinema ad filmed by *Chariots of Fire* director Hugh Hudson depicting a chameleon in a golden, sun-scorched desert. But everyone knew it was for B&H.

And this is the core of aspirational brands; you buy the pack or the advertising or other aspects of the marketing communication. There comes a point where the product barely seems to matter.

At the other end of the price spectrum the same can be said of many cars. Given that, for most people, these are the most expensive things they buy apart from their home this is really quite staggering. But look at any piece of car promotion, even today, and it's amazing how little actual information there is, let alone any meaningful

One Hard Question

comparison with other rival makes.

Which is rather odd, given that arguably the most famous ad in history, and the one that is often credited with provoking the creative 'revolution' we've been talking about, is a 1960 US ad for Volkswagen's Beetle, an ad that majored on its candid, 'here are the facts' point of view. The press ad by New York agency Doyle Dane Bernbach was called 'Lemon' because, in contrast to its flashy and glamorous rivals in the US car market, the VW was small and ugly. And, to add to its problems, it was, of course, the Hitler-mobile, still Adolf Hitler's 'people's car' to many Americans who had only finished fighting the Germans 15 years previously.

Undeterred, DDB produced a black-and-white press ad with an unvarnished photograph of an unlovely Beetle and a lot of copy. At the height of the era of so-called car industry 'planned obsolescence' it spoke lovingly about VW's commitment to quality and value, through describing the activities of a Beetle quality control inspector, Kurt Kroner (who may well have been fictitious). 'This preoccupation with detail means the VW lasts longer and requires less maintenance, by and large, than other cars. (It also means a used VW depreciates less than any other car).'

Note the 'by and large' – not too many hostages to fortune there. But, for the time, this tone was genuinely disarming and a timely reminder that many of those other big things with four wheels and tailfins broke down almost as soon as they were sold. And that there was nothing intrinsically shameful about considering the resale value of the car you bought. 'We pluck the lemons,' it concluded, 'you get the plums.'

DDB head Bill Bernbach, who wrote Lemon, once said, 'All of us who professionally use the mass media are the shapers of society. We can vulgarise that society. We can brutalise it. Or we can help it onto a higher level.' This was quite high-falutin' stuff but it helped to inspire generations of admen, particularly creatives. And, initially anyway, more in London than New York, where DDB was still regarded as distinctly odd.

At the same time as this was going on in advertising, a similar revolution, again inspired in America but taking root strongly in the UK, was happening in graphic art. America provided most of the famous artists of the 1950s and early 1960s, from Jackson Pollock to Roy Lichtenstein and Andy Warhol. In the commercial sector illustrator Saul Bass pioneered a stark, German-influenced graphic style that figured on famous posters (and later animated title credits) for films including *Love in the Afternoon*, *The Man with the Golden Arm* and *The Shining*. Movie posters and credits may have provided the initial outlet but press ads and posters followed rapidly as inspired students poured out of art colleges and found their way into advertising.

And there was a similar wave in architecture where the disciples of Frank Lloyd Wright and Frank Gehry set off on the roller coaster of self-styled modernist architecture. Eventually they would meet the graphic artists and designers and begin, among other projects, the often fraught large-scale revamping of the British high street. And some, including in London, Michael Peters, Rodney Fitch and the godfather of the gang, Terence Conran, would begin defining what still stands for good taste for most people today.

So it was all happening and, even though these creatives were inspired by art and (in Bill Bernbach's version anyway) truth, many of them found their most productive outlet marketing aspirational brands, where the communication often bore very little obvious relationship to the product reality. On the other hand their ads were often funny and entertaining (and certainly didn't shout at you in the way they once had) and, just like their contemporaries' designs, added greatly to the gaiety of the nation.

And the brands that worked best answered the one hard question, 'How can I connect with people in a crowded and sometimes anti-commercial marketplace?'

All brands depend to a greater or lesser degree on mnemonics, visual or audible signals that help us remember them (thus the controversy over so-called subliminal advertising, discussed earlier).

The usual 1960s and 70s solution was a memorable jingle, everything from the glutinous 'Hands that do dishes can be soft as your face' for Fairy Liquid to the somewhat implausible 'That's the wonder of Woolworths' for the now-defunct store group. Advertisers felt happy with these because, in some instances anyway, they worked. They were less sure about some of the comedy vignettes being produced by the new, trendier ad agencies.

One advertiser who decided to have it both ways was Anthony Simonds-Gooding, then marketing director and later boss of brewers Whitbread. Whitbread's main brands then were Whitbread Tankard and Trophy, two pasteurised keg beers, and the Dutch Heineken lager, brewed under licence in the UK. Keg beers, fizzy with a 'big head', ruled the roost then with cask-conditioned real ales on the verge of extinction. Lager was the coming thing, with the same attributes of easy-to-keep fizziness but a continental heritage (however ersatz some of the brands were). Lager was definitely more aspirational than keg beer.

To advertise Tankard and Trophy Simonds-Gooding enlisted the aid of the Allen Brady and Marsh (ABM) agency, famous for its brazen salesmanship (one of the founders Peter Marsh was a former actor who had moved on to a more productive stage). Another founder was creative director Rod Allen, known as 'the jingle king'. Allen produced 'The wonder of Woollies', 'This is the age of the train' for British Rail and the rather sweet 'Triangular honey from triangular bees' for Toblerone, among many others.

For Whitbread Trophy he offered, 'Whitbread, big head, Trophy bitter, the pint that thinks it's a quart'. This said it all really. It did indeed have a big head and, as Whitbread's 'value' brand, offered a lot for your money. And you remembered the ad or the jingle, even if it made you lurch for the off-button on the TV.

For Heineken, Simonds-Gooding went to the polar opposite of

ABM, Collett Dickenson Pearce, the cool agency where the young Charles Saatchi (and other luminaries like David Puttnam, Alan Parker and Hugh Hudson) had toiled.

CDP was then run by a young account handler called Frank Lowe, even though the three founders, ex-army men who were probably a little bewildered by some of their staff, were still around. Lowe was a zealot for what he, and many others at the time, was sure was great creative work (in creative departments there are only two sorts of ad, great and 'crap').

But Heineken proved a tough nut to crack and, in desperation, Lowe hauled in one of his top copywriters, Terry Lovelock, and dispatched him to Morocco on a thinking expedition with orders not to return until he had a Heineken campaign. Lovelock thought and thought, to the extent that many in the agency believed he had been abducted or just fled in fear of returning to face the music. Eventually the prodigal returned to suggest the campaign, 'Heineken refreshes the parts other beers cannot reach'. This was not greeted with unalloyed admiration but it was all they had so it was eventually put to the client who suggested, as clients do, that consumers should be asked what they thought via a number of focus groups of consumers.

Agencies hate focus groups as they claim that consumers only say they like what they already know. So anything radically new is almost bound to fail and, to no one's great surprise, Heineken did. But Lowe who, almost uniquely among account men, was not afraid to stand up to clients and browbeat them into doing what he wanted, stood by the campaign and Simonds-Gooding, who had a high regard for Lowe, decided to give it a chance.

And the rest, as they say, is history. 'Refreshes the parts' became one of the most famous and highly awarded campaigns of all time and Whitbread found itself with the brand leader in the fastest-growing and most profitable sector of the market.

But were people buying the advertising or the product? Clearly the campaign wouldn't have worked if the product had tasted foul but such lagers then, as mostly now, weren't the original continental brew but a rather lacklustre British copy. They were certainly buying the 'brand', a combination of the product *and* its message rather than simply the product. The jokes in the campaign, like the policeman's feet or the Sloane Ranger trying to learn to speak cockney, had become the mnemonic.

And this was a trick that Lowe and Simonds-Gooding were to repeat when Lowe went off to form his own agency in the 1980s, Lowe Howard-Spink, with partner Geoff Howard-Spink.

Lowe Howard-Spink launched Stella Artois in the UK for Whitbread, one of the first strong continental-type lagers (when Stella was first introduced into the UK it was imported from Belgium and you did indeed fall over after a few pints). Lowe ran a series of commercials loosely based on the French films *Jean de Florette* and *Manon des Sources* starring legendary French actor Yves Montand, with the line (or mnemonic) 'reassuringly expensive'. And Stella promptly became not just the best-selling premium lager but also the best-selling lager of all. It only began to lose its lustre when new owner InBev reduced its price to compete with cut-price supermarket lagers. People seem to have actually preferred it when it cost more.

Like many brands before, Stella appealed to a certain snobbery in consumers and a desire to be cool. But by leavening the message with humour, it persuaded people that it was OK to think this way. Many observers would say this is a British thing, that such an approach doesn't work so well in the US or continental Europe, let alone the rest of the world, where responding to advertising is said to be a rather more left side of the brain activity.

But, in the UK at least, the hard question was asked and some brands at least came up with remarkably successful and durable answers.

4

Even Further into the Beginning

The properties of the products we call brands – a motivating, distinctive truth that connects with and, sometimes, inspires people – didn't magically appear with the formation of Procter & Gamble in 1837.

And the wizards who deployed and exploited these properties (interestingly P&G's logo looks like a wizard, which has made it unpopular over the years with various religious types) didn't just emerge when brand managers hove into view after 1925 and the McElroy memo.

The great religions of the world are, in many respects, peerless brands. Christianity, Islam, Judaism, Hinduism, Confucianism and Buddhism, all emerged from modest beginnings to command the loyalty of, eventually, hundreds of millions of people. And they would delight even a brand manager's financial director by demonstrating steady growth (more or less) on a low cost and maintenance base.

Just as the language of marketing borrows from the military, with companies launching campaigns and trying to win the battle for market share, it also borrows heavily from religion. Famous brands these days are often called 'icons' after the simple but compelling images used to adorn Russian Orthodox churches. The term is over-used but, in so far as it indicates the ability to condense and communicate many values in a simple and memorable image, it is accurate shorthand for what marketing communications seek to do and the durability they seek to create. And, of course, an icon is also a work of art. So, in a way, the icon painters were the art directors of their day.

One doesn't want to push this analogy too far but all religious

One Hard Question

art is in some way propagandist; it's trying to get across a religious or spiritual or moral message via the visual image. And, after the classical age of Greece and Rome, nearly all art, in the West anyway, was religious in intent until the Renaissance. At about this time, in the mid 15th century and thereafter, some others recognised the power of these images and sought to exploit them to burnish their own brand image.

The main such group included monarchs and other rulers who commissioned the artists of the day to paint them in all their heroic glory. The Medici, the ruling family of Florence, were quick to harness the explosion of artistic talent in the Renaissance to their own purposes, chiefly persuading their unruly subjects that they were, really, the right people to govern them. At first these pictures of rulers would show them in various heroic guises, usually as part of a scene from classical legend. Then, just as clients today are always keen to make the company logo bigger and more prominent, these rulers began to cut out all the mythical stuff (which nobody believed had anything to do with them) and so the art of portraiture was born.

Holbein's famous paintings of Henry VIII are a classic case in point. Here is Henry, the dominant, rather fierce-looking monarch (downright unpleasant we might think, with modern eyes), cowing his subjects. Of course by this time, the early part of the 16th century, realism was beginning to creep in to painting and maybe Henry looked at these and thought Mr Holbein wasn't being quite flattering enough. Anyway, the great portraitist kept his head.

But Henry had his own marketing battles to fight, in particular his sponsorship of the Reformation in England, his adoption of the Protestant variety of Christianity over Catholicism. Henry had to ask himself a hard question when the Pope turned down his request for a divorce from his Spanish wife Catherine of Aragon (who had previously been married to his late brother), who was unable to bear him a male heir. An 'heir and a spare' was even more important to monarchs in those days than it is in 21st century

Even Further into the Beginning

Britain (so our monarchy is a pretty enduring brand too, despite its many vicissitudes).

What was Henry to do? Well he chose the nuclear option by embracing Protestantism, the faith devised originally by rebel priest Martin Luther in Germany. This meant that he could say he was no longer subject to the decrees of the pope in Rome and, so that no-one could be in any doubt, he appointed himself head of the church in England for good measure. These measures cleared the way for Henry to take five more wives (the second of whom gave birth to a male heir, Edward VI, who died aged 15). But it brought England to the brink of civil war, with Henry savagely suppressing the Pilgrimage of Grace, a revolt by northern Catholics, set England at odds with many powerful enemies, chiefly Philip II of Catholic Spain, and led to centuries of state-sponsored discrimination against Catholics in what became Great Britain.

So it was important for the Tudors, Henry's dynasty, to present themselves to their subjects, most of whom had been perfectly happy as Catholics, as glorious rulers, a lustrous brand. And they succeeded in so doing. Holbein may have been worryingly realistic but when Henry's daughter, Elizabeth I, eventually ascended the throne the copywriters and art directors of the day went into overdrive to hymn the praises of the 'Virgin Queen' or 'Gloriana' and her plucky little island, described by John of Gaunt in Shakespeare's *Richard II* as, 'this sceptred isle... this precious stone set in the silver sea.' Gaunt also made the point that the silver sea acted as a moat as well and the precious stone was also a fortress. So even Shakespeare was at it, promoting the party line (or the brand) in what appeared on the surface to be an account of history.

By this time the hard question to be asked had moved on a bit; it was no longer 'How do I get a divorce and produce a male heir?' Daughter Elizabeth was doing pretty well on her own as it happened, but now the question was 'How do we survive against the might of Catholic Europe?' But the image-making of the Elizabethan age

One Hard Question

lives on, just as Elizabeth's plucky country did. Even though life then could be nasty, brutish and short (as philosopher Thomas Hobbes described it in the 17th century), succeeding generations of historians, including one-time household name A.L. Rowse, harked back to a golden Elizabethan age. This reached a pitch in the austere post-war era of the early 1950s when Elizabeth II ascended the throne.

Neither the first churchmen or even Henry VIII decided to just create a brand, as modern marketers do (although Lorenzo de Medici perhaps did). But movers and shakers in any walk of life need to ask themselves hard questions from time to time – how do I produce a male heir? how do I solve this business problem? how do I survive?

Again, in contrast with today's marketers, who are armed with vast amounts of information about each and every market and the supposed needs of consumers (arguably too much in many instances), the answer to their questions may be sitting under their noses, be the consequence of dire necessity or simply the result of a happy accident.

Sony owes much of its success with the world-beating Walkman personal stereo to Masaru Ibuka, its founder and, by the 1970s, honorary chairman. On long airline journeys he would relax with Sony's only product in the market, the TC-D5 tape recorder, which was excellent but heavy, impossible for everyday use and expensive (not that this was a concern for Ibuka). So he got the tape recorder division to create a smaller version for him to use on his journeys. The engineers took their Pressman product, a large heavy cassette recorder that was used mainly by journalists for interviews and modified it, removing the recording function and adding stereo sound.

At the time the tape recorder division was in the doldrums. Few people wanted its expensive top of the market products and there was competition in the mass market from products like boom boxes, which left the company with little room for development in this area and casting around for future direction. But Akio Morita, Sony's legendary chairman, spotted the potential of Ibuka's pet toy and

Even Further into the Beginning

encouraged his engineers to develop a similar player, only cheaper and even lighter, that would appeal to the primary music audience, the youth market.

Naming the product was a problem. The head of the division, Kozo Ohsone, suggested the Walkman, but initially his colleagues didn't think it would work. The name sounded too prosaic as if it were a direct translation from the Japanese, but since no one could come up with anything else that they preferred, the brand name remained.

Then Morita was concerned that the headphones were too big and heavy and so wouldn't interest the young and active. At more than 400 grams they weighed more than the player and resembled a pair of earmuffs - not quite the chic look they were after. However another Sony division had designed a pair of lightweight earphones a few years earlier and these were adapted for the Walkman. These headphones weighed about 50 grams, were far less obtrusive, and so the listener could wander along playing his music without disturbing those around him.

The company was then faced with another hard question: how to market the Walkman in the face of critical and media scepticism, even ridicule. Some people said no one would want a tape recorder that didn't record while others said the market wasn't there, pointing out that the top-selling personal tape recorder of the time had sold only 15,000 units. So Sony gave media promotion a secondary role and went straight to the potential market. The company distributed the player to young people and celebrities around Japan, to gain user recommendation and build word-of-mouth testimonials. Instead of a conventional press launch, the press was taken on a tour through Tokyo where they could see actors displaying and listening to the Walkman.

The Walkman sold out a month after it launched, and was being purchased by all sections of society, not just the young. As preparations were made for launching round the world concerns

One Hard Question

about the name reappeared and the marketing department came up with new brand names for the US, the UK and Sweden. Then on a visit to Paris, Morita was asked by the children of Sony employees where they could get their Walkman, and that decided the question of the name for good. Within ten years 50 million Walkmans were sold and Sony's competitors had all plunged in with their own products. By answering their own hard questions ('How do we make better use of our own technological resources?' 'How do we connect to the key youth music sector?') Sony managed to invent the personal audio market.

'Necessity is the mother of invention' is a truth that goes all the way back to the Egyptian storyteller Aesop, who narrated how crows dropped stones into a pitcher of water until the level rose high enough for them to drink (a story confirmed in 2009 by scientists in Cambridge working with some ravens).

This was certainly the driver behind the pioneering bagless vacuum cleaner developed by James Dyson, who, but for his frustrations when trying to clean his house, would have been known, if at all, for the invention of a new type of wheelbarrow, the Ballbarrow.

Vacuuming one night, Dyson found that new bags in the machine worked only for a short time before he was, as he put it, 'just pushing dust around the room'. At the same time he had bigger but similar problems at his Ballbarrow plant. He had to stop the production line every hour or so to remove the spare epoxy powder that was sprayed on to the barrow to provide a tough form of paint. Naturally some of the powder missed the barrow and this was collected on a screen behind which was a fan, in other words a suction device similar to a vacuum cleaner. Yet the screen had to be regularly cleaned of powder particles thus stopping production.

Dyson was told by the powder spray firm that to do the job efficiently he needed a cyclone, a cone about ten metres high that spun the powder away by centrifugal force. They offered to make one for him for £75,000 and told him he could review one at a sawmill, where cyclones were usually installed. Dyson visited a nearby sawmill and decided he could build one for himself. It was when he'd completed the working prototype that he suddenly remembered his frustrating evening doing the domestic chores. Again he built his own crude prototype and found that it worked.

Five years and more than 5,000 prototypes later Dyson had the model he could bring to market. In 1983 he launched it in Japan, as no one in Britain would manufacture or distribute it since it would destabilise the valuable replacement bag market. The G-Force, as it was called, was designed in bright pink, setting the tone for the stylish designs of future products. The later DCO1 in grey and yellow had a NASA look to it, matching hi-tech design to the pioneering engineering. When he finally launched in the UK, after excellent results in Japan and the US, Dyson found that sales were slower than expected. Confronting the question of how to find and communicate the motivating truth to the consumer, Dyson insisted on returning to see-through bins so that people could see how much dirt and dust they were collecting. Previously retailers had persuaded him to put smoked-glass bins on the machine on the premise that consumers didn't want to see the nasty rubbish that had been residing on their carpets.

In tandem with his advertising agency of the time, Dyson also promoted the cleaners with the proposition that consumers could do away with bags, instead of the previous emphasis on suction efficiency. This proved the breakthrough, which meant the market had come full circle: the introduction of the disposable bag had previously been a big step up in convenience for the market.

Finally, the other manufacturers, which had wanted to keep Dyson out of the market, began to manufacture their own version of bagless machines. Nevertheless Dyson achieved market leadership in the US and the UK by inventing a brand with a real motivating truth, defining it as a compelling proposition in the marketplace and delivering that truth to the consumer.

One Hard Question

Sometimes companies don't have to dig at all to discover the hard question. It's forced on them by the market and they realise they have to change or go under. This is what happened to IBM in the 1990s, after decades of dominating the world computer market. In fact its control was so absolute that it generated that rueful expression in corporate purchasing departments: 'No one ever got fired for buying IBM.'

The company had built its success on the technological excellence of its mainframe computers and in 1981 it launched the IBM PC, banking on the brand reputation of its mainframes. This was the first computer to be bought not by corporate computer departments but by middle and senior managers, who were reassured by the IBM name. The security, confidence and quality offered by IBM meant that at one point in this era it earned 70 per cent of the worldwide computer industry's profits and in 1990 it reached a peak when it achieved the highest profits in its history.

Then it was hit by the drop in demand for mainframes, still a vital component of its business, as companies moved to the microprocessing systems and PCs that could do the same job, while at the same time a recession meant that corporate downsizing and budget reduction was in full swing. Just three years after its record profits, IBM set another record, with an $8.1 billion loss, then the largest single year corporate loss in US history.

The enormous growth in the PC sector driven by a host of new and nimbler competitors such as Dell and Compaq had changed consumer perception. PCs were now starting to be regarded as a reliable, cheap commodity, in which case there was no need to pay extra for the IBM name. Despite maintaining superb technological excellence the company had become bloated, bureaucratic, inflexible and remote from its customers. One critic compared IBM to a music publishing company run by deaf people. It was facing more massive losses and seemed far too out of touch with the marketplace to be able to make a comeback.

Even Further into the Beginning

IBM's hard question was: 'How do we survive in a market that has changed beyond recognition?' The answer was provided by Lou Gerstner, a former McKinsey consultant and turnaround expert with no technological background, who became CEO of the company in 1993.

Gerstner focused IBM's energies on two prime company strengths that had been neglected in the previous complacent and confused years. One was IBM's technological excellence. In the year after he arrived, IBM filed for more patents than any other company in the US and in the following years it pioneered new advances in voice recognition, supercomputer speeds, semiconductors and nanotechnology.

The second change was to return to IBM's tradition for excellent, if expensive, service. Gerstner re-integrated the company's major divisions, which had been split into autonomous business units, moved the company away from components and hardware and towards software and all-round IT services. IBM bought the Lotus software firm to help build up its software group and later acquired the professional services consulting arm of PricewaterhouseCoopers.

Increasingly IBM focused on business consulting, services and software as well as high-value chips and hardware technologies. This enabled it to win worldwide contracts from global groups in which it combined technological innovation with focused business solutions.

It also maintained its patent generation, being awarded more US patents than any other company in most of the last 15 years. This has turned its protection of IBM's intellectual property into a business in its own right, generating billions of dollars from other companies seeking to use its technology.

Just two years after Gerstner arrived, the company made a $3 billion profit on revenues of $60 billion, and while IBM has since ridden the ups and downs of the world economy like any other company, it has maintained Gerstner's business focus and continues as a healthy, vibrant company. And it sold its PC business to the Chinese.

By recognising that while customers didn't want a highly priced IBM PC they still valued the company's technological engineering skills and reputation for service, IBM was able to reinvent itself and communicate the truth about its proposition in a credible way to the marketplace. In essence this is what saved it from extinction.

5

Pile It High or Just Sell It?

One of the supposed benefits of brands is that they sell at a premium because customers are happy to pay a bit more for something they know and love.

And, to an extent, we will pay a bit more for the right brand. But these days brand owners don't just need to concentrate their efforts on sweet talking consumers, because they have another huge challenge on their hands, the power of mega-retailers.

In the days of yore the big retailers were department stores, very often upscale like Bloomingdales in the United States and Harrods in the UK. The emphasis, as it was across the shopkeeping spectrum, was on service as much as product and price. But at the lower end of the spectrum, street markets and the like, traders had always known that price mattered. Marks & Spencer began as a penny market stall in Leeds in 1884. The first big retailer to invade the high street on both sides of the Atlantic with such an offer was Woolworth. For decades it was the world's most successful and profitable retailer.

But another factor was looming. In 1916 one Clarence Saunders opened his first Piggly Wiggly Store in Memphis, Tennessee. This is thought to have been the first self-service grocery store. The trend caught on and gained strength in the US as the 1920s turned into the depression years of the 1930s and millions of people, many of them impoverished, sought value where they could find it.

On 4 August 1930 Michael Cullen opened what is thought to have been the first grocery supermarket in the Queens district of New York, King Cullen. Conventional grocery store chains including Krogers and Safeway eventually saw the need to compete and formed

One Hard Question

what became national supermarket chains. Krogers was the first to see the benefit of a supermarket surrounded by a parking lot.

In the 1960s these and others were rapidly overtaken by Sam Walton's chain of massive discount stores, Wal-Mart. Walton too started in a modest way, in Bentonville Arkansas, but his stores, which sold everything from chewing gum to guns, met the needs of Americans in the increasingly mobile 1960s and 70s. Wal-Mart, which also owns Sam's Club warehouses, is now the biggest retailer in the world, although its business is largely confined to North and South America, with its ownership of Asda in the UK being the main exception.

In the UK the first self-service grocery store is thought to have been Sainsbury's in Croydon in 1950. The first Sainsbury's shop was opened in Drury Lane between Holborn and Covent Garden, then a poor part of London, in 1869. It sold mainly dairy products, which in those days were as likely to make you ill as nourish you, and rapidly built up a reputation for 'quality and value', the food retailing mantra to this day. By 1922 it was the UK's biggest grocery retailer and remained so until 1995, when it was overtaken by Tesco.

Tesco itself had begun as Jack Cohen's market stall in the East End of London in 1919, taking the name Tesco when Cohen bought a shipment of tea from T.E. Stockwell in 1924 and added the first two letters of his surname to the tea supplier's TES. Cohen opened his first high street grocery store in Edgware, north London in 1929 and lost out narrowly to Sainsbury's in the self-service stakes by opening his first such shop in St Albans in 1951. But supermarkets proper took a long time to arrive. Sainsbury's still operated some shops in which your bacon and cheese were hand-sliced by a fatherly figure in a white coat well into the 1960s.

Through the 1970s and 1980s Sainsbury's stayed ahead of Tesco, which was derided by some for its 'pile it high, sell it cheap' philosophy (the early US model) and, later, dependence on Green Shield trading stamps which it adopted to drive sales. These offered you gifts from a catalogue if you secured enough stamps by shopping at Tesco regularly.

Sainsbury's was the middle-class, or aspiring, choice and the Sainsbury's brand was driven by the perception of better quality than its rivals (just as it had been in 1869), summed up by its long-lasting slogan 'Good food costs less at Sainsbury's'.

These developments impacted brand owners in several ways. The growth of supermarkets, particularly on out-of-town sites with ample parking, introduced the habit of the weekly shop and so brand owners (household goods as well as food products) had no alternative but to be in these stores, at discounted prices or not.

And the supermarkets were quick to see that their buying power could force even the biggest brand owners to cut their wholesale prices and even pay to be displayed in store. The supermarkets, Sainsbury's in particular, began to offer their 'own label', later 'own brand', products. These were cheaper versions of the brand owner products, usually manufactured by the brand owners themselves for the supermarkets. The supermarket orders were so big that few manufacturers felt brave enough to turn them down, even though they were hurting their own sales in the process.

Brand owners were therefore competing with good quality own brands, which had no need for costly advertising. Indeed they were very often forced to make a sizeable contribution to the supermarkets' own ad campaigns when their own products were featured. So their old ability to sell at a premium thanks to the platform created by spending millions on advertising was sharply eroded.

A further development, and one that is still being played out today, was the overwhelming importance of in-store display. Supermarkets stock only so many brands in a certain sector, apart from their own of course. So brands need to earn prime display positions, which are reviewed regularly. At Tesco, for example, the most profitable brands are displayed at the top of the counter, the least profitable (as far as Tesco is concerned) on the bottom shelves where you have to search for them.

So in-store became a medium in itself, either through promotions (which, again, the brand owner would fund) or packaging, to create stand-out attractive products.

The one hard question now facing brand owners was, 'How can I preserve my margins, and therefore profit, when somebody else is doing my marketing for me (often with my money)?'

For the supermarkets the issue was, 'How can I make money at all when customers continually expect even cheaper prices?'

For brand owners the answer is often scale, the realisation that if they become big enough, and rich enough, then the supermarkets will have to deal with them on equal terms or risk losing big-selling branded products which consumers, despite all the blandishments of supermarket own brands, still buy in prodigious amounts. So the past two decades have seen companies like Procter & Gamble, Unilever, Reckitt Benckiser (the household goods giant), Nestlé and Kraft snap up their rivals at a ferocious rate.

The confectionery market, for example, used to consist of a huge number of small and medium-sized companies. In England we had the Quaker trio of Cadbury in Bournville, a suburb of Birmingham, and Rowntree and Terry's in York. Quite why the upright people of the Quaker faith took to chocolate, by the way, remains a mystery. Some say it's because it's an alternative indulgence to the demon drink.

But in 2010 Kraft snapped up Cadbury to add to Terry's and the Swiss chocolate brand Tobler that it already owned, while Rowntree has long since been swallowed by Nestlé. To customers it seems ludicrous that companies the size of Cadbury, and before it, Rowntree, are deemed too small to survive in the modern world. And maybe the customers are right. But the reason many analysts and investors think they are too small is the rampaging power of the supermarkets. But even the mighty Tesco, with around 30 per cent of the UK grocery market, worth some £40 billion in sales, needs a working business relationship with companies as

Pile It High or Just Sell It?

big as Kraft and Nestlé.

And some brands still dominate, whatever the supermarkets may try to do on their own account. P&G paid $57 billion for shaving brand Gillette in 2005, not just to be bigger or to move into a new sector but to gain control of a brand that dominated its market and enjoyed the kind of margins that just aren't available in food or household products. Since P&G bought the brand it has grown even stronger, with its new Fusion razor, which is eye-wateringly expensive for a so-called 'everyday' purchase, reaching $1 billion in sales faster than any other P&G product in history. Gillette now enjoys what is virtually a monopoly in the branded shaving market, with rival Wilkinson Sword, now owned by a German company Energizer Holdings, a poor second and the rest (not that there are very many of them) nowhere.

And giant companies can still afford to spend enough on advertising and marketing to retain their place in consumers' affections. P&G, as reported in Chapter 2, is the world's biggest advertiser and rival Unilever isn't far behind.

A relative newcomer (to the world stage at least) Reckitt Benckiser, the product of a merger between the Dutch detergent company Benckiser and British food and household products group Reckitt & Colman, is giving the two giants a run for their money in household products with its own aggressive programme of product innovation backed by heavy advertising for its stable of brands ranging from Strepsils throat lozenges (which it bought from Boots) to cleaning product Domestos. Reckitt Benckiser has recently renamed itself RB, a rather dull move for a company that owns brands like the exotic-sounding Cillit Bang (another cleaner).

So most successful brands have stayed with the formula that has seen them through good, and sometimes not so good, times, the discovery and heavyweight promotion of a motivating, distinctive truth that connects with consumers.

But the great change forced by the supermarkets is that there are

One Hard Question

now far fewer major brand owners. To survive you have to be big enough to ensure that nobody can afford to de-list you.

For supermarkets one hard question used to be, 'How can I stand for both quality and value?' since the big groups always seemed to stand for one or the other. Sainsbury's, as we've seen, profited for years from its platform of offering the best quality in the volume grocery business. It might not have been quite as cheap, or sometimes nearly as cheap, as Tesco but it offered an acceptable combination of quality, price and convenience.

Tesco, on the other hand, was regarded as cheap but depressingly cheerless. It was a down-market option and that mattered in the class-conscious UK. But in 1973 Ian MacLaurin, who had been the company's first management trainee in 1959, took over from Cohen family member Leslie Porter as managing director. MacLaurin promptly ditched Green Shield trading stamps and put the money saved into price cuts and massive improvements to the distribution chain. In 1977 he launched 'Operation Checkout', the UK's biggest price-cutting programme, and followed this five years later with a second burst, both designed to put pressure on market leader Sainsbury's, which was unwilling or unable to cut its prices and margins by a similar amount. But Tesco still had a poor brand image.

In 1982 Tesco appointed our old friend Frank Lowe, formerly of CDP and Heineken fame, and his new agency Lowe Howard-Spink to handle its advertising. This was unexpected in the extreme; prior to this Tesco had run exactly the kind of price-bashing advertising you would expect, created by the McCann-Erickson and then Saatchi & Saatchi agencies. But Lowe wasn't having any of this, or rather he offered something else besides. This was a bold attempt to re-position Tesco as offering our old friends quality and value – by emphasising quality. So he signed up comedian Dudley Moore, once of Oxbridge revue *Beyond the Fringe* and then part of a cutting-edge comedy team with Peter Cook, also originally of Fringe fame. At the time Moore was already a big star (he went on to star in Hollywood films such as

10 with Bo Derek) but still of a decidedly up-market flavour. About the last person you'd expect to see in a Tesco ad despite his humble origins in Dagenham.

At the time Sainsbury's was running a popular campaign devised by copywriter David Abbott featuring celebrities cooking and tasting its products. One such was former Chancellor of the Exchequer Denis Healey (it's usually a sign that a campaign is running out of legs when you put a politician in it). Moore would have fitted into this very well. But Lowe didn't do anything as boring as show Moore shopping at Tesco or eating its food. Instead it had him chasing free-range chickens around the French countryside to show the lengths to which Tesco buyers went to source the best produce. Now history doesn't tell us how many French free-range chickens or their eggs made it into Tesco stores but the campaign made a statement – that Tesco had changed and it was now safe for the middle classes to shop there.

And Tesco sales and market share grew rapidly, overtaking the by now struggling Sainsbury's, where a number of bosses had tried and failed to make its flagging distribution system work, and leaving other smaller chains such as Safeway (no relation then to the American version) far in its wake.

In these circumstances, particularly after the price-cutting Operation Checkout offensives, the natural thing for a company to do is to try to improve margins and grow by opening new stores, both of which Tesco succeeded in doing. But two important rivals were emerging in the north of England: Asda, a spin-off from the struggling Associated Dairies business in Leeds, and family-owned Morrisons from Bradford. Both fought on a price platform, the hardy perennial in the supermarket or, indeed, any other retail business.

Asda expanded apace under the dynamic duo of former McKinsey consultant Archie Norman and former Mars marketer Alan Leighton. It managed to undercut even Tesco's prices, in part due to the lower operating costs of its huge stores based primarily in northern England where land was relatively cheap. Eventually it was to sell out to Wal-

Mart, which had hitherto failed in its efforts to invade Europe, falling spectacularly foul of discounters like Aldi and Lidl in a vain attempt to establish itself in Germany.

Morrisons, also based in Yorkshire, was a much older business than Asda but it began to expand rapidly under Ken Morrison, majoring on its own no-nonsense offer and some fresh food innovations including well-stocked fresh fish counters which, at the time, none of its rivals bothered with. Morrisons eventually bought Safeway to expand in the south of England.

All these companies, together with a now revitalised Sainsbury's under former Marks & Spencer food boss Justin King, were big enough to grind down costs, including the prices paid to suppliers, although they were (and are) much smaller than Tesco.

Tesco was also coming under pressure from consumer groups who claimed it was dominating a number of so-called 'Tesco towns' in the UK by either opening new stores in an area where they were already dominant or buying spare land so that its rivals couldn't compete.

There was also pressure on the supermarket sector as a whole because of its alleged harsh treatment of suppliers and the pressure low prices were applying to traditional shops in the high street. The latter criticism the supermarket giants answered in their own inimitable way, by opening up their own smaller high street shops, Tesco Metros and Extras and Sainsbury's Locals. This was not exactly what the critics had in mind but customers evidently thought otherwise.

But, with a market share approaching 30 per cent and restrictions on new stores in the UK, Tesco had a hard question of its own to ask: 'How (and where) can we keep growing?'

And the answer was – abroad.

Retail businesses of all hues have found overseas expansion a headache. Woolworth managed to export its cheap and cheerful formula successfully from the US to the UK for a number of years but you don't see Bloomingdales or Macys in the UK. Neither did

Pile It High or Just Sell It?

you see Wal-Mart until it bought Asda ten years ago.

There are exceptions as always. The Spanish, with the Mango and Zara shops for young women, have introduced some supermarket principles – quality and value, slick distribution that allows them to change ranges rapidly to keep up with fashion – to the high street in the UK and elsewhere and profited mightily.

But food retailers tended to stay put. French giant Carrefour, the world's second-largest food retailer after Wal-Mart and just ahead of Tesco, has managed to plant the Tricolour in a number of countries although it has recently pulled back from some.

Undeterred, Tesco decided to have a go, beginning quietly in Eastern Europe where it still had to fight some of the big German discounters and the Dutch giant Ahold. Tesco sets great store by its operating model, a uniform way of running its business whatever local conditions may be, and, to date, it has succeeded in growing sizeable businesses in Eastern Europe (chiefly Poland) and Asian markets, including South Korea, China and Thailand. India is the current expansion target although local rules there make life difficult for overseas retailers. It has also ventured into the US, a notorious graveyard for British businesses of all kinds including retailers. It has opened several hundred Fresh & Easy convenience stores, a version of Tesco Extra, in California and the West Coast and the jury is still out on these.

Tesco says the shops are on target and it's just losing money (around £186 million in the year to February 2011) because the recession caused by the sub-prime housing market has hit particularly hard on the West Coast. Critics say that Americans don't like pre-packaged food products (the Tesco convenience formula) and Fresh & Easy will never work. But, away from the West Coast, Tesco's worldwide sales are growing by more than 25 per cent a year (aided by the continuing torrent of new stores) and international now accounts for about a third of Tesco's £60 billion turnover. So Tesco appears to have succeeded in finding a growth path by finding its own way of doing what its peers

One Hard Question

like P&G and Nestlé in the brand owner world have done, becoming bigger by expanding internationally.

But what of the other supermarkets? International expansion doesn't appear to be on any of their radars at the moment although other big UK retailers like Sir Philip Green's Top Shop and Marks & Spencer (again) have said they are looking abroad. The ever ebullient Green clearly thinks he can match the success of Mango and Zara while Sir Stuart Rose at Marks & Spencer has said he regrets the decision of his predecessors to pull out of European markets.

In its market leader pomp Sainsbury's acquired the Shaws chain of supermarkets in New England, now sold, and also launched the Homebase DIY chain, now also sold. In its current healthy state neither of these moves look that clever although Sainsbury's would doubtless say that it needed to spend all its effort and money restoring its core UK supermarkets business. So, in the short term at least, neither Sainsbury's nor Morrisons is likely to get its chequebook out, although Wal-Mart, which is having a 'good' recession in the US as its lower prices become even more attractive, may be tempted to take its Asda brand elsewhere in Europe.

The UK supermarkets, including Tesco, have sought to answer their one hard question about domestic growth in two ways: by expanding into non-food products and, in a noteworthy steal from the brand owners, launching premium brands. All the UK majors have been flirting with non-food, chiefly clothing and electrical products, for decades, with clothing proving a particularly hard nut to crack. At first glance these seem rather strange areas to move into; specialist retailers in these markets, by and large, are not as consistently profitable as the supermarkets, partly because sales of both clothing and electrical products suffer in a downturn. But the supermarkets, with the exception of Morrisons, which has so far stuck to food, clearly believe they have both the shop space and buying power to make a go of it.

And it was Asda, once a dairy company, which showed the way. In the early 1990s Archie Norman and Alan Leighton took their life in their hands and invited maverick fashion retailer George Davies to join them to create a clothing range. Davies, who learned his trade at the Liverpool-based retailer and mail order company Littlewoods, had shot to fame in the previous decade when he had transformed an unloved rainwear clothing chain called Kendalls into the high street and catalogue whiz kid Next. Although not a designer, not that he minds being taken for one, Davies has a perceptive eye for women's fashion and at Next had produced the so-called 'total look'; tops, bottoms and accessories that matched. He also saw the importance of a catalogue operation, a mainstay of Littlewoods, and the Next Directory brought catalogue shopping to a whole new market, away from its working-class northern roots.

But Davies liked to run the business his way and, like that other fashion maverick Sir Philip Green (who had been deposed as boss of a listed company called Amber Day), fell out with the City and the Next board as the froth of the 1980s stock market ebbed away.

But Norman and Leighton were never lacking in confidence and they set Davies loose creating his 'George' brand, virtually a business within a business, including some standalone shops. Asda had plenty of shop space and George revolutionised people's expectations of the clothes they could buy from a supermarket. And they were very cheap. Davies, who left Asda when Wal-Mart moved in, went on to turn the same trick with the rather more up-market Per Una range for Marks & Spencer and has recently launched his own retail and internet clothing business GIVe (*sic*).

Tesco, with brands including Florence and Fred and, rather more cautiously, Sainsbury's with Tu, followed in Asda's footsteps and now, rather like Dudley Moore's French chickens, it's OK for the middle classes to buy clothes from supermarkets.

With electricals it's a rather more straightforward story. The supermarkets have infinitely more buying power than the likes of

Comet and Currys and rapidly worked out that people would chuck a flat screen TV into their shopping trolley if it was cheap enough.

But what about food? Which is, after all, their staple business? Most of the UK supermarkets now offer three brand categories: value (i.e. cheap and sometimes not that good either), standard lines and up-market, for example, Finest at Tesco and Taste the Difference at Sainsbury's. Thus they are able to do exactly what most brand owners are not (although they used to able to): structure their brand ranges to satisfy both customers who want the cheapest prices and those who are prepared to pay a bit more for what they perceive to be a classier brand. Finest and Taste the Difference vary a bit; Tesco Finest has a greater proportion of ready meals. But they are heavyweight deliverers of margin, as are the supermarkets' organic foods. And shoppers who aren't interested can still find enough of what they want in the value and standard ranges.

A brand owner in the food sector just can't do this, or not on the same scale anyway. A confectioner might be able to offer a more upscale chocolate alongside its standard brand (as Cadbury began to do when it bought organic and fair trade maker Green & Black's) but it hardly works anywhere else. In a market like washing powder, manufacturers will have a brand or two that offer more alleged rocket science in the formulation at a premium but sooner or later competitive pressure from rivals will force the price back into line. But essentially a brand is a brand and, if it's going to sell in supermarkets (or even be listed) it has to offer both quality and value. Only the supermarkets can pick and choose how much quality and how much value they offer.

6
Beauty That's More Than Skin Deep

Brands distinguish themselves from their competitors by getting under the consumer's skin in so many different ways.

It may be that 'it does what it says on the tin' (Ronseal) or a Russian meerkat burbles on about a mix-up over websites (comparethemarket.com). Or perhaps it's a reputation for peerless engineering combined with a certain aspirational style (BMW). Yet with some businesses, it's the people and processes on the front line that must exemplify the brand's motivating truth every day or else the whole enterprise falls apart.

First Direct telephone and internet bank was built on that premise. In 1989 the then Midland Bank (later acquired by HSBC) grappled with the hard question of how to provide banking that matched the new economic, social and technological environment that its customers were operating in. At the time there was widespread disillusionment with and apathy towards the banking system. All the banks seemed the same. Many customers did not use branches at all and of those who did, customer satisfaction levels were relatively low. The 1980s boom in the UK had helped to produce a fast-paced, impatient lifestyle for many young people, especially young professionals. The common use of credit and debit cards, the advent of ATMs outside banks and the launch of mobile phone technology reinforced the general feeling that banks were behind the times with their ponderous procedures and old-fashioned offices.

Midland Bank set up First Direct to provide banking for the modern consumer. It offered round the clock telephone banking from a central location, 24 hours a day, seven days a week, 365 days a year.

One Hard Question

It was the first bank designed with the customer first and foremost in mind.

The proposition was clear and one with which bank customers could identify because it was speedy, convenient and available at any time of the day of week. But to achieve this First Direct had to build a set of clear core values. These were: responsiveness, openness, right first time, respect, contribution and the Japanese concept of *kaizen*, or continual improvement. Unlike many of the empty mission statements that companies issue these days, these values had to be lived and carried through for the bank to succeed.

Clearly in a business promising its customers so much more than its competitors and where millions of key transactions would take place one-to-one on the phone, quality of people and processes was paramount. Any error, technological or human, would destroy the brand's reputation instantly for that customer and probably for their friends and acquaintances.

The bank recruited people from social professions and customer-facing roles. They wanted people who could work fast and efficiently under pressure on the phone and on screen while maintaining warmth and sincerity with the customer. There was an intensive seven-week training course and staff had to pass a total of 54 accreditation tests in the first nine months of employment. This was all backed up with career development programmes and bonuses and other incentives to keep good people with the bank.

When talking to customers, staff could look at their accounts and account histories and so display a knowledge and understanding that gave a personal touch to the transaction. The system enabled them to deal with 85 per cent of all calls without having to transfer the customer to someone else, and call answering targets were to answer 75 per cent of all calls within 20 seconds or less.

This all added up to a very powerful proposition. People appreciated the time they saved and the inconvenience they avoided by using First Direct instead of going into a bank branch and also the speed and efficiency of the service. Paradoxically First Direct was able to offer a better service on the phone than its competitors provided face-to-face in their branches. It has regularly had the highest customer satisfaction ratings of any bank with, in 2006, 96 per cent of its customers being willing to recommend the bank to others and in 2008 new customers being referred to First Direct on average every eight seconds.

Part of this success was due to First Direct's recognition that it had to pay as much attention to the employee experience as the customer's. It introduced on-site massage, concierge car servicing and laundry and many other staff services and in 2006 was featured prominently in the *Sunday Times* list of the UK's 100 Best Companies to Work For.

The company launched internet banking in 1998, text message banking in 1999 and in 2004 First Directory, where additional services were added to current accounts such as free text message banking, annual travel insurance and mobile phone insurance for a fixed monthly charge. It also continued to add other new services to maintain its lead over the competition.

Changing accounts from one bank to another was a notoriously difficult and time-consuming process, especially with the growth in monthly direct debit payments from people's accounts. Banks had relied on this and the inertia factor to keep dissatisfied customers, who simply couldn't face the stress and time involved in moving to another bank. First Direct was the first bank to offer a 'one-click' option for transferring accounts, including standing orders and direct debits. Customers could now set this in motion by clicking one button on the website.

By 1994 the bank had reached break-even point and moved into profit the following year when it gained its 500,000th customer. Its innovative structure made its margins far higher than its conventional competitors. Quite apart from incurring no branch property costs, in 1996 it had 2,400 staff dealing with 640,000 customers, where a branch-based bank would have required at least 4,000 employees to handle that number. It now has more than one million customers.

The success of First Direct was a triumph of insightful branding strategy and execution. Midland answered its hard question with a radical offer that both met customers' current needs at the time but also showed them what the future could be like. It also recognised that the brand faced another hard question. Would its people and processes be strong enough to deliver the brand proposition and not let a brilliant idea wither away in the execution? The subsequent satisfaction ratings and word-of-mouth recommendation levels demonstrate how First Direct was able to embed its brand promise and values deep within every aspect of the organisation.

The banking and mobile phone markets don't have a lot in common, except that to the layman they are both complex and intimidating. This 'deterrent factor' in the phone market provided an opening for Charles Dunstone, who had set up the Carphone Warehouse in 1989 as an operation to sell in-car phones to the consumers (mainly young) who were attracted by the new portability of these exciting gadgets. For a while he had little or no competition and then as the product changed from a car phone to a personal phone and a stream of large multinationals moved into the market, Dunstone had to confront his hard question: 'How can my business stand out in this complex and fast-moving market where both manufacturers and service providers are competing for control and bombarding the consumer with conflicting messages?'

His answer was to provide an independent and reliable source of advice to potential users. The Carphone Warehouse would be not just a distributor/retailer but would also provide an informed guide to the buying decision of the purchaser.

As with First Direct, the quality of the staff was crucial to the success of the company. Carphone Warehouse had to build trust, mainly among mobile phone users, but also among manufacturers and service suppliers. So Dunstone needed employees who were expert in the products and the needs of the customers but also embodied the company's values. The principle was that at the Carphone Warehouse products and services were bought, not sold.

Dunstone summed up the company's operating philosophy in five clear principles:

- If we don't look after the customer, someone else will
- Nothing is gained by winning an argument but losing a customer
- Always deliver what we promise. If in doubt, underpromise and overdeliver
- Always treat customers as we ourselves would like to be treated
- The reputation of the whole company is in the hands of each individual.

It's worth noting that these principles are down-to-earth descriptions of ideal behaviour rather than the usual abstract corporate values.

Carphone Warehouse was offering customers a very attractive proposition. They could go to one shop, which stocked all the main phone brands and models, and be guided through this difficult selection process by an adviser who was committed to providing the product that best suited the customer's needs. The employee had to deliver the brand promise. If the customer didn't feel that he'd had the best advice and got the right product, no amount of advertising, PR or design would compensate for the employee's failure.

In its recruitment process Carphone Warehouse looked for well-qualified and highly motivated people from a wide range of backgrounds. Diversity was important because Dunstone wanted to match his staff to the spectrum of potential customers. The business gained a higher proportion of graduate recruits than any other retail business, with an important role in selection being given to local shops so that they could meet candidates and ensure local teams maintained their cohesion.

Training was rigorous, both centrally and locally, and based on the five principles mentioned earlier. In fact the company would typically invest four times the industry average on training. New employees had to undergo two weeks intensive training and a rigorous assessment before being allowed into a shop. They were encouraged continually to upgrade their knowledge of IT and communications equipment and services.

To match its belief in the customer being the heart of the process Carphone Warehouse developed its own proprietary process which mirrored customers' real needs and was designed to train staff in relating to a wide range of customers: young or old, IT-smart or total beginner. Dunstone also allowed staff the latitude to offer customers the best possible deal, with managers given the leeway to price tactically to fight off local competition. All were paid a good basic salary to avoid temptations to favour any one supplier.

In another move to emphasise the supremacy of the customer and therefore the importance of the front line staff, Carphone Warehouse called its head office the Support Centre and kept its design and fittings lean and functional. Resources were focused on the front line stores and staff, and all aspects of the customer experience.

The power of the Carphone Warehouse brand enabled Dunstone to move into fixed-line services through its TalkTalk brand and also into broadband. It is now Europe's leading independent mobile communications retailer with operations in 11 countries and it moved into the FTSE 100 Index of leading shares in 2007. Throughout this expansion, Dunstone has maintained his principle that the performance of his people is fundamental to the brand. Only by continually emphasising that the staff must support and express the brand's motivating truth has he been able to maintain the company's reputation for excellence and hence its growth.

Technological innovation always opens up space for new brands, a fact that First Direct and Carphone Warehouse were able to exploit, even though their success depended as much, if not more, on the quality of their people as on new systems and pieces of kit. But how do you bring something different to the table when you enter a market where the basic product was invented, by the Earl of Sandwich, 250 years ago?

In 1986 two college friends, Julian Metcalfe and Sinclair Beecham, thought the quality of sandwiches on offer in London could definitely be improved. The products were good but not great, and they had a vision of a lunchtime shop for workers where the food would be wonderful and also good for you – with fresh ingredients and no additives. The hard question was how to bring a new distinctive sandwich chain into a mature, highly competitive market with thousands of privately owned outlets at one end and the mighty Marks and Spencer at the other.

Metcalfe had a two-pronged answer: improve the sandwich-making process so as to provide better products, and entrust the selling process to highly motivated staff enthused with his own passion for food.

Metcalfe was fanatical about the quality of his food and learning from the ground up how to satisfy his customers' requirements. He and Beecham spent four years just running the first Pret A Manger sandwich shop in Victoria while they tested and refined their products and systems. During this period, which might be called a rather long research and testing programme, they focused on serving the very best food and organising the most efficient system for meeting the peak lunchtime demand. They weren't in a hurry. Metcalfe took eight months to decide on the best Cheddar cheese and four years perfecting the chocolate brownies.

When the time came to expand, the key decision they made was to have all sandwiches made at the shops where they were sold, from fresh ingredients dropped off at the locations by their suppliers. In that way they distinguished themselves from the major chains where the products are made at a central depot and distributed to the stores. They were aiming for the best of both worlds. Fresh food made that

One Hard Question

day at the shop but to a standardised recipe so that a crayfish and rocket sandwich would taste as good wherever it was bought. And they used cardboard packaging to emphasise that the food had to be eaten that day and could not be kept overnight. All leftover food went to charity each night.

Recruitment and training was organised with the same painstaking attention to detail. Pret A Manger searched for people with the same energy, enthusiasm and genuine interest in the business as the founders. Only one in 14 applicants would be accepted and all candidates had to work in store for a day after which the store's employees would vote on whether they should be hired or not.

Metcalfe set up a policy of keeping in touch with customers and staff. He encouraged customers to contact him with praise, blame and ideas and whenever a customer wrote in to praise a staff member Pret would award that employee with a star from Tiffany's made of real silver plus a personal letter of thanks from Metcalfe himself.

Throughout their expansion Pret has been very careful to go for quality of growth rather than quantity, refusing to go the franchising route, for example, and maintaining their core business in London. There are now about 263 stores, most of them in London, and in 2008 (after its McDonald's diversion) Pret was sold to Goldman Sachs and a private equity fund for £345 million, with Metcalfe and the management retaining a 25 per cent stake.

Often it's identifying the *right* question that is the hard part of the process. Metcalfe and Beecham proved that by doing this people can move into a crowded market and create a fresh new brand, simply by applying a passion for excellence to the process of making and selling a better version of a basic product.

Sometimes the hard question is simply a fork in the road. Which way should a brand under pressure go to avoid an inevitable decline?

At the start of the 1980s the iconic US brand Harley Davidson was under attack from Japanese motorcycle manufacturers, who were making lighter, cheaper, better-engineered models that were starting to make inroads into Harley Davidson's core market. The company had a choice between accepting that the motorbike market was changing and so taking the Japanese on at their own game or returning to their core values and building on the strong loyalty and appeal that the brand still attracted.

Harley Davidson recognised that there was still enormous potential in the brand's values of freedom, individualism, enjoyment and the way it represented the great American dream of getting out on the open road away from all the pressures of modern life. So rather than follow the rest of the market, they decided to emphasise the 'retro' quality of both the products and the brand's values. They stayed in the heavyweight (750 cc and above) sector of the market and introduced new models all with the traditional styling.

While they had work to do on restoring product quality – partly achieved by bringing in foreign parts and technical improvements – the management recognised that it was the attitudes of the company's employees and customers that were also key components of the brand's health.

They opened dialogues with the employees and the Harley Owners' Group (HOG), which had been set up a few years earlier but never properly utilised. They eliminated rafts of company management levels, turning instead to self-directed teams and established intensive training, with each employee receiving 80 hours a year, plus three-day training courses for dealers.

They put large investments of time and money into HOG, with events and regular communications to the extent that by 2001 it numbered 660,000 in 115 countries and now has over one million members. The average Harley owner is now likely to be in his or her 40s and an accountant or corporate lawyer rather than a tattooed Hell's Angel lifted from the 50s film, *The Wild Ones*. The number of people returning to Harley after years away from the brand has increased by a factor of three since the 1980s while a year-old Harley costs 25 per cent more than a new one and there are waiting lists for new Harleys. Group members spend 30 per cent more than non-members and the brand makes 20 per cent of its revenues from non-motorbike related sales – holidays, events, clothing and other merchandising.

The overall effect is of belonging to a club of shared values with the bikes at the hub of the experience. A typical weekend rally, which all the senior management attend, will attract 25,000 owners. Besides building customer engagement and reinforcing the brand, these events allow Harley to keep in touch with the changing needs of their customers and combat competitive threats.

The renewed focus on core values among staff and customers had a powerful effect on the business, with the company recording record revenues and income for 16 consecutive years. In 2008 it hit $5 billion revenues with net profits over $1 billion.

Other companies that have gained success through making their people and processes the focus of their brand include FedEx, the largest express courier firm in the world. Founded by Fred Smith in 1971, FedEx has been built on service and 'reliability with a friendly face'. Hiring the right people, putting them in charge and letting them build the systems around them has been the key to gaining the lead in what had become a commoditised market.

The FedEx approach relies on the employees' commitment to the brand and their inbuilt customer focus, with most managers being promoted from front line jobs. 'In a service company like ours, the perception of quality is influenced every time an employee interacts with a customer,' Smith has said. Clearly he's of a like mind with Charles Dunstone.

The company has also had the foresight to realise that customer service works on the macro as well as the micro scale. It set up a huge distribution centre near Memphis to provide an instant depot for its large clients and has also installed computer terminals in the offices of 100,000 customers. At the distribution centre FedEx would keep supplies of urgently needed items such as computer components so that they could be dispatched to the customer after just one quick phone call. And the company has managed to install computerised systems which can track the delivery vans minute by minute without alienating the couriers, who get immediate feedback on their performance once they get back to base.

It's clear that focusing people and processes to provide the best possible customer service works for both large and small companies. In fact this is often how small firms grow to be very large indeed.

7

The Medium Is The Message

William Lever, later ennobled as the first Viscount Leverhulme, was a soapmaker from Bolton who, like his rivals in Cincinnati at Procter & Gamble, set great store by advertising and marketing. Something of a control freak (he built his own town Port Sunlight in Lancashire to house his workers) he still found advertising frustrating. And he is alleged to have commented, 'I know that half my advertising money is wasted. The problem is I don't know which half.'

This has been a frequent lament of advertisers down the ages, one hard question that they've signally been unable to answer. They know that advertising is a very effective way of reaching consumers and building sales. But it is frequently lambasted as a scattergun approach, wasteful and expensive even if effective.

This applies to all conventional advertising media, press and magazine ads, radio and posters, as well as the most expensive medium of the lot – television. So advertisers have sought other means of promoting their wares and they're particularly attracted to media they find easy to measure. Which is why direct mail, the stuff that cascades through your letterbox, remains popular despite the senders knowing that most of it is discarded. A response rate of just 2 per cent is regarded as a good result by most direct mailers.

And the internet has profited mightily in recent years, particularly in the UK, because it's the most easily measurable medium of all, particularly paid-for search where agencies use all manner of wheezes to move their clients to the top of Google pages.

But what do we mean by medium and the media?

Well one rather lumpen dictionary definition describes a medium as 'an intervening substance through which impressions are conveyed to senses, etc.' This is actually quite useful. It talks about impressions rather than information, which helps to explain why some of the 'aspirational' campaigns described earlier worked so well. And it implies that the media are a collection of intervening substances, so that includes things like packaging and point of sale display, which occupy the space between seller and buyer.

The most effective, and cheapest, medium has always been word of mouth, of course, personal recommendation. But most advertisers realise that they have to kick-start and then sustain this happy state of affairs. Which means dipping into their pockets from time to time as people are, regrettably, fickle creatures.

But why is it so hard to measure certain media like television? Television audiences are actually measured relentlessly by a variety of researchers. Advertisers don't just buy airtime and sit back and hope for the best. In the UK anyway they don't actually buy airtime, they buy impacts. They will know from the researchers and the TV stations which groups of people watch certain programmes (left-handed housewives in Bolton or whatever) and pay accordingly to reach a given number of them. If the TV station doesn't deliver the promised impacts in an agreed amount of time it will have to pay some money back or hand over extra airtime.

But, and this problem still remains, how do you know your target audience is responding to your campaign? Sometimes you can measure this by sales but at other times, and for many non-retail product advertisers, this is impossible. Brand awareness is another measure but does it actually do you any good?

The people who operate this system on behalf of the advertisers are called media planners and buyers. Increasingly these days we get media 'strategists' too. Once upon a time, when there were fewer media, advertising agencies used to be responsible for this. As such they were called full service, creating the ads and then placing them in the media. They often offered other services too such as research and public relations, sometimes for no extra charge.

This was made possible because, as we mentioned briefly earlier, they would earn generous amounts of commission from the media owners – 10 per cent usually in the press, 15 per cent from TV. Some media owners, for example poster companies, used to pay even more (and still do, but not to the ad agency). By some amazing act of osmosis agencies usually managed to increase their rate of commission charged to the client on most media to a chunky 17.65 per cent. Ultimately, of course, it was the advertiser's money. This was paid to the media owner who then gave an agreed percentage of it back to the agency.

So, even though the agency would be managed by account handlers (mostly) and would pay the highest wages to the creatives, the copywriters and art directors who created the ads, the people who actually kept the wheels of commerce turning were the agency's media staff, who tried to ensure that the client's money reached its target and appropriate results were achieved.

These people came from all kinds of background but were regarded as a rather rough lot, the equivalent of the Essex-born traders in the City who used to occupy the trading floor of the Stock Exchange. All they needed to be was numerate. These days some City traders earn vast fortunes, never move far from their computers and wouldn't know the way to the floor of the Stock Exchange. And the same is partly true of some media people.

How did this come about?

The media men in agencies (they were nearly all male in those days) became fed up with their lowly station. Even though the top media man would enjoy the title of media director and sit on the agency board, they still, by and large, felt under-appreciated. They would moan that, when the agency was making a new business presentation to a client, they would be on last and, if the presentation overran, never get on at all. Silly, no doubt, but it seemed to sum up a prevailing lack of respect and regard. And theirs was an undeniably important function, as we noted earlier.

So in 1971 Paul Green, a media manager at the big Garland-Compton agency and a maverick by nature, decided to set up his own company which he called, reasonably enough, Media Buying Services. The name actually came from a Canadian company with which Green had an arrangement but while such a company doing such things had caused few ripples in Canada it prompted a veritable tsunami in the UK.

At the time commission rates for agencies were fixed by an agreement between the Incorporated Society of British Advertisers and the Institute of Practitioners in Advertising (the agencies). When Green popped up, going straight to advertisers and saying, 'I'll buy your media better and cheaper in return for some of the agency commission', many in the advertising establishment would have cheerfully tarred and feathered him and run him out of town.

But advertisers too had grown restless (to a degree, like Lord Leverhulme, they always had been) because the price of television advertising in particular had rocketed in the UK in the 1970s and 80s.

Commercial television had come to the UK in 1955, decades after it had first appeared in the US. The first ad to be shown on ITV was for Gibbs SR toothpaste. Gibbs SR was owned by the mighty Unilever, itself the result of a merger in 1930 between Lord Leverhulme's Lever Brothers and a Dutch outfit called Margarine Unie. Both companies used vast amounts of palm oil from West Africa in their products. And as commercial television grew to challenge the press as the biggest advertising medium it was the likes of Unilever (which today owns brands like Hellmann's and PG Tips as well as its soaps and margarines), P&G and the big brewers and retailers who dominated the commercial airwaves.

For many years these were licensed solely to ITV, a federation of regional broadcasters. These included Granada in the northwest, ATV then Central in the Midlands, and Thames on London weekdays with London Weekend Television taking over from Friday

The Medium Is The Message

evening to Sunday. And commercial television, consisting as it did of regional broadcast monopolies, was, as Canadian Lord Thomson, the owner of Scottish TV put it, 'a licence to print money'.

ITV's monopoly wasn't broken until Channel 4 arrived in 1982. Channel 4 was and is a publicly funded broadcaster whose remit is to provide the kind of 'minority' programming (however that may be defined) not found on ITV. As such it took a while to build an audience and an advertising market (in the early days its ads were sold by the understandably unenthusiastic ITV regional sales forces).

But the ITV companies carried on printing money, the more so as in the 1980s numerous other advertisers discovered the attractions of TV advertising. These included entities such as the then state-owned British Rail (the Government's Central Office of Information which handled government advertising until its recent closure used to be just about the biggest TV advertiser today), car companies, banks, utilities like the newly privatised British Gas and British Telecom, the supermarket giants and even stock market darlings such as the Hanson Trust industrial conglomerate.

All this conspired to force up the price of prime airtime, much to the displeasure of the traditional brand owners, hitherto the mainstay of commercial television. So Green's message (and he was soon joined by people like Chris Ingram with his company Chris Ingram Associates, or CIA, and The Media Department which became TMD and later Carat) didn't fall on deaf ears, although the likes of Unilever and P&G stuck cautiously with their full service agencies for a while longer.

And there were other changes afoot.

1973 saw the debut of LBC, a news radio station for London and the UK's first legal commercial radio station. It was shortly followed by music station Capital and then by a mixture of news and music radio stations across the country (the music ones did rather better).

Although it's fair to say that commercial radio (the home of the first 'soap operas' in the US) has disappointed its enthusiasts in the UK by failing to challenge the BBC successfully or generate substantial ad revenues, it gave clients and the new media agencies something else to think about.

But the real revolution in media (and real competition for ITV) came with new technology. In the first instance this was via the privately owned Astra satellite which made it possible for pay-TV operators to broadcast to the UK alongside the BBC, ITV and Channel 4. Initially there were two such companies, British Satellite Broadcasting (a consortium of *Financial Times* publisher Pearson, French investor Chargeurs and ITV company Granada) and Rupert Murdoch's Sky Television. These merged in 1990 to form BSkyB with Murdoch having the whip hand. In time other so-called digital channels entered the market, buying space on the BSkyB platform and also competing for ads.

And throughout the 1990s roads across the UK were enthusiastically excavated as a gaggle of cable TV operators were allowed to dig into the market, eventually coming down to two, NTL and Telewest. In 2006 they merged under the Virgin Media banner when Virgin owner Sir Richard Branson rolled in his mobile business to create the UK's first 'convergent' media company offering paid-for cable TV, fixed and mobile telephony and broadband.

ITV meanwhile had gone through a series of mergers of its own, ending up with new London seven-day operator Carlton and the venerable Granada carving up the land between them. They merged to form ITV PLC in 2004.

And, of course, we had the internet. For its first few years website owners struggled to attract advertising (as, to an extent, they still do) but the rise of Google created the category of paid-for search (in essence employing an agency to devise stratagems to get your name and message to the top of Google search pages).

All this choice, though bewildering, should have been great news for advertisers. Competition, after all, is supposed to be a good thing for customers. But advertisers still had to ask themselves the same old hard question: 'Will the motivating truth of my brand stand out credibly and consistently in its chosen medium or media? And how do I select those media?'

At one time the media choice had been TV for most advertisers with a big budget and a choice of other media for those without. Most big advertisers used TV with a range of back-up media. These often included the press for retail offers and posters as a way of extending the life of TV messages rather more cheaply.

But more media competition meant that some once-reliable audiences declined. In the UK ITV, which in its regional heyday had often delivered audiences of between 10 and 20 million for programmes like *Coronation Street*, came under pressure.

It now had to compete with Channel 4, Sky and numerous smaller channels which, although they didn't win large audiences themselves, still served to chip away at ITV's hegemony.

The BBC discovered the merits (or so it thought) of aggressive scheduling under leaders such as Greg Dyke and Michael Grade, both former ITV executives. With a huge licence fee settlement of around £3 billion the Beeb, and Sky, now gaining huge pay TV revenues from its Premier League contract, were much wealthier than ITV, whose revenues were foundering because advertisers were looking elsewhere.

Direct mail, as we've noted, became popular because its results could be measured even though they were often nothing to write home about. Internet search advertising rapidly became highly popular for the same reason.

All of a sudden certain 'communities' on the internet such as MySpace, YouTube and Facebook began to develop huge audiences and advertisers began to turn their attention to exploiting these.

And, of course, there were serried ranks of media men eager to help them explore these new opportunities, with the ubiquitous media strategists making a handsome living from trying to predict what was around the next media corner.

We'll look at internet communities in more detail later because they do appear to be changing the nature of brand promotion and even consumers in general in fundamental ways.

But brand owners found themselves in even more of a pickle than before. All this choice was a pain because audiences were fragmenting, tried and tested media were losing audience and share and consumers were migrating to places where they were hard to reach (in the case of the BBC, impossible to reach by ads).

Most theories of brand promotion assume that you have to dominate a certain medium to thrive. And, if you can't dominate it, at least you have to be noticed. This applies as much to in-store display as anywhere else. You may have the world's most creative and attractive packaging and a great product but it won't do you much good unless you can afford to blag or buy your way onto the supermarket shelf.

Many brand owners had thrived mightily by sustaining a consistent presence on prime time ITV but that had become harder to do as pressures mounted to do more in stores, build an online presence and chase young or upmarket audiences (ideally both, of course) on to Channel 4 or into more niche media. But some brand owners discovered ways of doing things differently, often, it has to be said, without the invaluable advice of the media men. This often happened if they didn't have much money to spend.

In 1984 Apple brought out its first Macintosh personal computer. Company founder Steve Jobs had always been intent on going his own way (declining to sell his software separately for example, as Microsoft's Bill Gates was beginning to do to great effect). The first Mac needed to make a big splash so Apple hired celebrated film director Ridley Scott to make a commercial. Earlier in his career Scott had worked mainly as a commercials director after art college and a stint as a BBC director. He had directed the famous 1974 Hovis ad, filmed in picturesque Shaftesbury, Dorset, to the tune of Dvorak's *New World Symphony*. By 1984 he was much in demand as a film director although he has continued, like his Hollywood director brother Tony, to make commercials from time to time.

Three creatives at the Chiat Day agency on the West Coast of America, Lee Clow, Steve Hayden and Brent Thomas, had the very bright idea of making an ad themed on George Orwell's *1984* for the Mac computer, launching in 1984. The theme they chose was 'saving the world from conformity', possibly Bill Gates and Microsoft. So Scott's ad showed a spectacular blonde athlete Anya Major racing up an auditorium to smash a screen displaying a Big Brother-like dictator with a hammer. Major's somewhat striking tank top was pristine Apple white.

The ad is famous for a number of reasons, one being that it is widely thought to have only aired once, in the third quarter of 1984's Super Bowl. But in fact it ran twice, the cunning agency sliding it into a little-watched show in Idaho late the previous year to make sure it was eligible for the following year's ad awards.

Even airing only in the Super Bowl, America's most-watched programme, is a mind-bogglingly expensive business costing millions. The commercial itself cost $1.5 million to make, a staggering amount for the time. But that was it for 1984 in terms of paid-for airtime although it became such a cause célèbre that it was aired many times for free. Many cinema owners showed it with the trailers.

And it was absolutely perfect for Apple. Even when Apple struggled in the years to come, ditching founder Steve Jobs for a decade before he returned in triumph to launch the iPod and iPhone, it had established itself as a brand with a motivating distinctive truth in a way that its much larger opponent Microsoft, for all its success, signally failed to do.

Yet, to achieve such ends, it had spent relatively little on advertising.

Many advertisers have tried to pull off this trick since and very few have succeeded. But Apple's strategy has been widely copied nonetheless as advertisers seek to gain commercial impact through their ads becoming an event in themselves. This is clearly much cheaper than impressing yourself on the public by bombarding them with ads you've paid for but a rather more hit and miss affair.

Recently though, commercials budgets have started to go through the roof again, after many years in the doldrums, as some advertisers have gambled on making striking films (and sometimes so-called internet-only 'virals') that may appear to have very little to do with the product, apart from maybe the voiceover and the end frame, but find their way on to YouTube and the like. Sometimes advertisers will make a relatively long film of a minute or three for the YouTube audience and use a cheaper 30-second cut-down for paid-for broadcast. Guinness uses this tactic to some effect.

But what you don't get out of this is a campaign, a series of linked promotions that build interest in the brand through the way it develops over a number of episodes.

This approach goes all the way back in the UK to the Oxo TV 'family' with what seemed like generations of women producing an endless range of dishes for their appreciative families thanks to the ubiquitous stock cube. Shorter series can work brilliantly too; one famous example was CDP's campaign with Joan Collins and the late Leonard Rossiter for Cinzano. Each of the ads featuring Rossiter accidentally pouring a drink over the Hollywood actress Collins still raises a smile.

These days such extended campaigns, apart from the most cheap and cheerful, are a rarity. Lowe Howard-Spink produced a number with Prunella Scales as Dottie and Jane Horrocks as her daughter for Tesco.

Microsoft's Bill Gates, clearly peeved by the nerd who appeared in Apple's ads and looked rather like him, tried to fight back with a campaign featuring him and comedian Jerry Seinfeld. Shortly afterwards the agency Crispin Porter lost the business.

But let's go back to 1984. Apple asked itself one hard question: 'How can we launch this strange product successfully, one that's different to all the other computers out there, even though we don't have enough money to launch a heavyweight campaign?'

And the answer was to spend a fortune (a sum of money that, at the time, was beyond just about every advertiser in the world) on a single commercial and run it just once (if you discount Idaho). Which, at the time, broke every rule in the marketing textbook.

As we've seen, this stroke of genius didn't really help other brand owners trying to make their rather more substantial budgets go further.

But, of course, not every brand is an Apple.

8
The Consumer Is Not a Moron, She's Your Wife

Before the brothers Saatchi hove into the world's consciousness after helping Margaret Thatcher's Tories with the 1979 General Election, David Ogilvy was the world's most famous adman.

A peerless copywriter and salesman, Ogilvy had begun his career in marketing working for George Gallup's Audience Research Institute in New Jersey after emigrating from Britain to the US in 1938. Gallup, of Gallup Poll fame, was beginning to revolutionise marketing and advertising with his belief that consumer behaviour could be predicted accurately using his methods.

This chimed with Ogilvy's thinking; one of the aphorisms ascribed to him was 'I prefer the discipline of knowledge to the anarchy of ignorance.' When he opened his Madison Avenue ad agency in 1952 he took the title of research director.

Ogilvy had a business problem to solve. He was 41, an Englishman on Madison Avenue (although he liked to think of himself as Scottish), trying to launch his own agency after a varied career as a chef in Paris, an Aga cooker salesman, a brief time in a London agency working for his brother Francis and research at Gallup. Francis was now running Mather & Crowther in London and backed brother David with a small amount of cash. But he needed to make a mark fast and, as many British-owned agencies after him, including Saatchi & Saatchi, would be subsequently able to testify, butting into Madison Avenue was no easy task.

The one hard question he asked was 'How can I find a point of difference?' This question, of course, has been asked by brands of all hues down the ages but Ogilvy came up with an answer perfectly in tune with his own thoughts and beliefs.

It was that the function of advertising was to sell and that this should be based on information about the brand and the consumer. Advertising should be believable.

Now nearly all advertising had always aspired to this. Rosser Reeves, a contemporary of Ogilvy's, was seeking his 'unique selling proposition', Procter & Gamble was still looking for a decisive advantage in all its products and emphasising this in its advertising. But consumers, customers, were still largely thought to be a canvas comprising people on which brands could paint any picture they liked through persuasion, or outright hucksterism.

However another Ogilvy saying was 'There are now unmistakable signs of a trend in favour of superior products at premium prices. The consumer is not a moron, she is your wife.' Although Ogilvy and Mather, as the agency became, ended up as one of the biggest in the world (it's now owned by WPP Group) with massive clients like Unilever and Shell, the Brit on Madison Avenue built his reputation on niche brands, many of them British.

His most famous line was for Rolls-Royce, 'At 60 miles an hour the loudest noise in this new Rolls-Royce comes from the electric clock.' This was witty, engaging and true. It may not have been the most important thing about such an expensive car but it was a brilliant way of pointing out that it was quieter than all the others, a point not lost on Hollywood stars and producers who queued up to buy them.

He invented 'The man in the Hathaway' shirt, a cool dude with an eye patch, hinting at acts of derring-do in the services somewhere, a potent reference in the 1950s.

He introduced Commander Whitehead, an elegant bearded Brit, to sell Schweppes tonic in the US. Later on, when the agency was motoring like the aforementioned Rolls-Royce, he pointed out that Unilever's Dove soap was 'one-quarter moisturising cream'.

All these campaigns took one aspect of the brand and majored on that rather than battering consumers with a barrage of 'X is best'.

The Consumer Is Not a Moron, She's Your Wife

Ogilvy's agency was arguably the first to try to ensure that its advertising found a way to make consumers *believe* that the brand would deliver its promise. Even Mrs Ogilvy would have found any of these propositions hard to dispute.

In so doing Ogilvy let a monstrous world-conquering cat out of the bag.

There isn't a company out there today that doesn't claim it is 'customer-centric,' that all its actions, such as moving call centres to Asia or charging you extra if you don't pay your bills online are solely predicated on customer satisfaction and service.

Even governments have caught on. 'Ruritania has no truck with illegal methods of interrogation and torture and puts the well-being of its citizens first at all times,' Ruritania will say as incriminating documents are shredded and hapless prisoners are shunted off to ever-darker and more remote dungeons.

This isn't Ogilvy's fault of course and he would laugh today if he could (he died in 1999) at such developments, but trying to get people to believe in brands as well as just putting them in their shopping basket (Ogilvy's primary intention) can easily turn into a rogue's charter.

And never more so than in politics.

Fast forward to the autumn of 1978 and Britain is expecting a general election to be called at any moment. Prime Minister Jim Callaghan's government is only able to muster a majority of MPs by allying with the Liberals, and the country, as it had been for years, is beset by strikes and (modestly) rising unemployment. And Margaret Thatcher has just taken over as leader of the Conservative Party.

The Tories had been early adopters of advertising in elections, hiring the agency Colman Prentis and Varley in the late 1950s. Labour had picked up the gauntlet in the 1960s, running its famous 'Yesterday's men' ad knocking Ted Heath's Tories in 1970 (Heath won). The Tories had always had a sprinkling of admen in their ranks and Thatcher was persuaded to award the Tory advertising account

One Hard Question

to Saatchi & Saatchi, an upstart agency that was already beginning to challenge the establishment of US-owned J Walter Thompson and Ogilvy Benson & Mather (as Ogilvy's agency was now called in London).

Charles Saatchi was highly dubious about this political lark, recognising the potential for publicity but fearful that by handling the Tories, then behind in the opinion polls, the agency would attract more bad publicity than good. But younger brother Maurice and Tim Bell, the agency's charismatic managing director, were both convinced Tories and persuaded Charles that the appointment would really put the agency on the map, making it famous with the public as well as clients. This, they reasoned, would greatly assist their strategy of world domination so Charles was reluctantly persuaded.

One reason agencies were leery of political accounts was that political parties didn't have any money. At elections they received free party political broadcasts but the rest of the promotion effort went on the cheap medium of posters. The Tories had always received a number of free poster sites from friends in industry, particularly cigarette companies who were big users of posters in those days, having been banned from TV.

And the incumbent government has a big advantage in elections; it's free to name whatever date it likes so long as it's within five years of the last one. So the opposition parties need to nurse their slender ad budgets carefully to make sure they still have enough in the pot for the actual election period.

Back in 1978 most people thought Jim Callaghan would call an election in the autumn. He was ahead in the polls and everyone expected strikes and unemployment to get worse over the winter (they were right). As things turned out 'Sunny Jim' held on (governments always thinks that things can only get better) but the Tories began their ad campaign in the autumn nevertheless.

Copywriter Andrew Rutherford and art director Martyn Walsh decided to major on aspects of the country that irritated and

The Consumer Is Not a Moron, She's Your Wife

frustrated people. Chief among these was the state of the National Health Service, a hardy election perennial. Puns are much favoured by copywriters, especially on posters where brevity is the key, and the favoured ad in the campaign (by the Tory leadership anyway) was 'Britain isn't getting better'. This was typical Saatchi, short, sharp and effective. Actually it was like a David Ogilvy ad, taking one simple point and making it strongly rather than over-claiming.

But Rutherford and Walsh had another favourite. This was a queue of the allegedly unemployed under the headline 'Labour isn't working'. Actually they weren't unemployed people at all but members of Hendon Young Conservatives who had been persuaded to turn up at the Welsh Harp reservoir in north London to have their pictures taken for some unexplained purpose. Unfortunately only 20 or so rather than the intended 100 had made it so Walsh had to take pictures of this rather small queue and then retouch it back in the studio to make it look much, much longer.

This is itself caused controversy when the ad became the centre of frantic attention, although it's a common enough wheeze these days. Some writers even maintained that the queue comprised Saatchi employees snaking along the pavement outside the agency's Charlotte Street offices.

The poster, rather like Apple's 1984 commercial, only appeared a few times and might well have been forgotten but it was given the precious oxygen of publicity by a furious Labour Party. News that the people in the posters were 'actors' had leaked and Chancellor of the Exchequer Denis Healey, a noted bruiser, thundered that the Tories had plumbed a new low by 'selling politics like soap powder'.

And there was much muttering, and barely-concealed anti-Semitism, about the bumptious Saatchi brothers (Sephardic Jews from Baghdad by birth) suborning precious British political traditions, just what Charles Saatchi had always feared.

Actually the mischief maker-in-chief was Tim Bell who went on to become Mrs Thatcher's key adviser, even down to her hairstyle allegedly. Maurice Saatchi eventually became an adviser too (both were subsequently ennobled by the Tories) while Charles tried to stay out of it. One story has him returning to his sixth floor eyrie in Charlotte Street only to realise that a meeting was taking place along the corridor with Mrs T and various minions. Then, horror of horrors, came the sound of a door opening. Saatchi never enjoyed meeting clients, particularly prime ministers in waiting (to this day he doesn't even turn up to the opening of his celebrated art exhibitions) so he is said to have grabbed a nearby mop and bucket and pretended to be the cleaner.

Anyway Margaret Thatcher and the Tories went on to win the election, eventually held in March the following year after the notorious 'winter of discontent', when the country was plagued by strikers who included dustmen and mortuary attendants.

And the Saatchis, and the buccaneering Bell, found themselves the most famous admen on the planet, going on to snaffle huge and prestigious accounts like British Airways and embarking on a spending spree, snapping up the mighty Ted Bates agency in New York and briefly becoming the biggest agency network in the world.

At one time they even contemplated an audacious bid for the stricken Midland Bank, arguing that it was a brand just like any other. This was a bridge too far and, not long after, the agency imploded, finding it owed too much in deferred payments for acquisitions as the financial temperature dropped sharply in the recession of the late 1980s (Bell had departed by then to set up his own business, initially with our old friend Frank Lowe).

But the supposed success of 'Labour isn't working', winning a British General Election no less, had persuaded advertisers all over the world (once again) that there was nothing you couldn't persuade people to do if they only believed.

Which was complete nonsense of course. 'Labour isn't working' was a clever and perfectly legitimate poster whose importance had been blown out of all proportion by Labour's foolish reaction to it.

The Consumer Is Not a Moron, She's Your Wife

All of a sudden advertising wasn't just advertising any more, the attempt to sell people something by persuading them it had value, but 'total communications'.

But did such an approach help consumers (and indeed voters) to believe that the brand in question could and would deliver its promise? This rapidly became the very hard question brands had to ask themselves. They were trying to reach consumers who were exceedingly savvy about advertising, marketing and selling. At the same time many people did (and still do today) really want to believe in the products they were buying. Concerns over health, ethics and sustainability began to influence absolutely everything from the purchase of food (free range and organic) to cosmetics and pharmaceuticals (health, testing and animals) to cars (carbon emissions, gas-guzzling so-called 'Chelsea tractors').

And very often it wasn't just the brand that was in question but the brand owner or the country and its political systems where the brand or product was produced.

Nestlé has fought a running battle with opponents of its artificial baby milk, sold mostly to mothers in the third world. Opponents say it's harmful and therefore exploitation. Nestlé says otherwise. You occasionally wonder why one of the biggest companies in the world bothers with such a product when it brings such grief. Nestlé's opponents would say it's because it makes loads of money out of it. Nestlé would say it's doing its bit to help poor people.

Nestlé, along with other companies, ran into the same kind of outrage for allegedly not paying coffee producers a fair price. This, of course, was one of the triggers for the fair trade movement. Now when you buy a jar of coffee it comes covered with more ethical advice than a packet of cigarettes.

Supermarkets found themselves running into trouble for a multitude of reasons: bullying suppliers, driving out small businesses, paying rock-bottom wages (Wal-Mart in the US is still being pilloried for this) or selling rubbish.

As ever the supermarkets have responded, for the most part, more nimbly than their brand owner rivals. For years supermarkets in the UK were criticised for dishing out billions of plastic bags a year, many of which found their way on to streets and into ponds and rivers and green spaces. They then bit the bullet and began to hand out free or cheap 'sustainable' bags (although charging anything for these still looks mean) and some niche players like Marks & Spencer began to charge for plastic bags in the food department.

The issue of sustainability has revolutionised the car industry with two of the three US car giants, Chrysler and General Motors, driven into bankruptcy by buyers switching elsewhere for smaller, cheaper, more environmentally friendly models. GM was, until very recently, the biggest car maker in the world but its emphasis on so-called sports utility vehicles (SUVs) and trucks (a few years ago more Americans bought trucks than cars) backfired as the price of gasoline soared and then the recession hit.

By contrast its Japanese rivals Honda and Toyota (Toyota is now the biggest producer) scored heavily with their more modest and more reliable offerings. The first really big-selling 'hybrid' car, the Toyota Prius, which runs on an electric engine until it hits a certain speed, set down a marker for the whole industry. Toyota, alas, has subsequently had its own road crash with a whole series of mechanical malfunctions which critics says it concealed. But it still sells lots of cars. Now, when you look at a car ad in a magazine, carbon emissions are all it tells you about. Nothing as useful as how fast it goes or the price.

Product packaging, which had come to be viewed as a promotional medium in its own right, with some packs and even brands being billboards in their own right – 'I can't believe it's not butter'– came under sustained fire (it had never been popular in some quarters) for the waste it produced.

In packaging, everything that couldn't be recycled became bad, which was gloomy news for a design industry that had managed to persuade brand owners they should be putting more of their effort

The Consumer Is Not a Moron, She's Your Wife

into luring customers at the point of sale. It's harder to shout from a hessian bag.

Most people these days think their energy suppliers are brazen frauds, exceeded only in their voracity by banks and other financial services providers.

The world of finance, of course, has always engaged what we used to call the consumerist movement, not without reason. Conditions vary across the world of course but, in the UK for example, the prevailing model of free banking for retail accounts has led to a proliferation of extravagant charges for things like exceeding your overdraft limit, even for a minute or two.

Banks hang on to money for far longer than they need to before paying it into accounts, so they can lend it out overnight to other banks. The performance of all the multiplicity of companies that invest your money is questionable as they extract high charges for frequently dismal (and occasionally disastrous or downright crooked) performance. Somehow or other the weight of regulation poured over these outfits never seems to make things any better.

And then, of course, we have only recently come through the credit crunch, the near-terminal banking collapse that began in the US as mortgage providers sold billions of dollars' worth of home loans to people who couldn't pay them back. The sellers were often intermediaries who got paid on sales not the performance of the mortgage. These mortgages were then bought by investment banks and sliced up and flogged on to millions of gullible institutions around the world, from the big retail banks to your local building society and local authority pension fund.

Because banks are supposed to hold a certain amount of asset backing in relation to their outstanding loans it came as the nastiest of shocks when they found these assets (the mortgage packages) were, in many cases, worthless.

Such problems were compounded by an era of extremely cheap money. It may not have seemed like that to you and me, and certainly

One Hard Question

not to any credit card holder who didn't pay off their balance each month, but interest rates around the world were at historic lows through the 'noughties' so people borrowed too much, particularly against property that soared in apparent value because it was so easy to get a big mortgage. This applied just as much to commercial property, offices and retail parks, for example, as to apartments and houses.

Another cheap money consequence was that the return on bank lending shrunk as competition in the sector increased because a range of financial operators found they could borrow money easily and cheaply. Banks make more money per loan if interest rates are high because the spread between the rate they borrow at and what they lend it at increases, even if the percentage difference is the same. So, in an era of cheap money, they sought investments that offered a better return and, as it says on the tin, better than average returns always carry higher than average risks. And US sub-prime mortgages, along with many other dodgy investments, offered mouth-watering returns as the hapless mortgagees (who didn't have the money in the first place) were paying way over the odds for their loans.

But it wasn't only the sub-prime cowboys who pushed their luck too far — everybody was at it.

The population of the country of Iceland is about 300,000 (about the size of Nottingham in the UK) and the nation's two biggest assets are the fish that surround it and its appeal to tourists. But in 2008 we had the bizarre situation in the UK that an Icelandic company called Baugur, sadly no more, owned a huge chunk of the British high street.

The company started life as a single Bonus supermarket in Reykjavik in 1989. It grew thereafter and merged with local department store Hagkaup to form Baugur in 1998. It then embarked on the shopping spree to end all shopping sprees in the UK by buying part or all of House of Fraser, Somerfield, Hamleys, Oasis, the jewellers

Goldsmiths, Karen Millen, Whistles, Austin Reed, Debenhams and Woolworth and a seeds and beans outfit called Julian Graves. Oh, and appropriately, Iceland frozen food.

This was made possible by huge loans, mainly from Icelandic bank Kaupthing, now also deceased. Kaupthing had a lot of money to lend because it promised depositors above-average interest rates, a kind offer taken up by many UK savers including the aforementioned local authorities and many charities.

When Kaupthing collapsed, taking Baugur with it, the UK government resorted to anti-terrorist legislation to freeze Kaupthing's assets in an attempt to get savers' money back. We mentioned the fictional Balkan state of Ruritania earlier in a different context but this was truly Ruritanian. So it's hardly a surprise that trust in financial institutions, even those still standing, is at all-time low despite the expenditure of many marketing millions to try to achieve the opposite.

David Ogilvy, who ushered us into this chapter, wanted his ads to be believable (although not necessarily to turn consumers into believers) and he did so, in part, by trying not to over-claim.

He thought it was better to say something accurate and believable about one aspect of a brand than make grandiose claims of behalf of everything.

But in the era of total communications, where even middling companies have one public relations firm to deal with the City, another to deal with consumers, corporate social responsibility departments (to try to keep the company on the straight and narrow or help persuade the world that it is) and numerous advisers ranging from investment bankers through management consultancies to advertising experts and others, the temptation is to try to tell the whole story, and the whole story is rarely without flaw.

And it's not just companies getting ahead of themselves. A vociferous minority of consumers also insists that companies, brand owners, are squeaky clean from top to bottom. As recent history tells us they aren't, nor are they likely to be.

Neither, of course, are the politicians. We'll examine them once more in the next chapter.

9

And So To (More) Politics

There's not much sentiment in a commercial brand transaction.

However much the customer may love and esteem their perfume, their car or their retailer, deep down they know that the brand's purpose is to extract as much money as possible from them over the greatest possible time. And the consumer is determined to get the best value from the brand at the lowest cost. It's a trade-off in which each party is hoping to gain an edge, however slight, over the other. Hence the intense time and effort that businesses put into their promotional strategies and the keen-eyed scrutiny that the consumer places on advertising claims, offers and price cuts.

Yet what about the immense selection of not-for-profit brands that need the consumer to buy in to their values, beliefs, policies and actions? 'We're not here to grow profits and give our shareholders a good return,' they say. 'We're here to make the world a better place.' Building and maintaining a not-for-profit brand can be a much more complex process than in the commercial world, where the transaction is a simple exchange of money for goods or services.

In the political arena it's often the case that people support a political party for many years and then find it's changed so much that it doesn't seem to reflect its core supporters' views or seems determined to lead them in a different direction. Conversely parties that don't show that they are adjusting to the changing world around them and the developing views and needs of the electorate will just wither away and die.

In the UK during the last two decades both the Labour and Conservative parties have had to confront hard questions as they found themselves increasingly out of touch with the electorate. They have had to rebrand themselves considerably, while promising that their core historic values are still intact.

In the 1990s, the Labour Party was in crisis. It had been out of power since 1979, after which there was the breakaway from its ranks of four top Labour politicians to form the Social Democratic Party and the Conservatives won continual dominance under Margaret Thatcher. Even in 1992, with the Tories in disarray and generally loathed by the electorate, Labour could not project itself strongly enough to win the public's confidence and it lost yet another election, despite dropping its policies of unilateral nuclear disarmament, re-nationalisation of all public utilities and strengthening of trade union rights.

The problem was that Labour had moved much too far from the centre ground which any political party which hopes to take power has to command. It was clear in 1992 that Labour was adjusting its positioning but it still had a long way to go.

Soon after the 1992 election the Conservative government ran into trouble when on Black Wednesday it was forced to take Britain out of the European Exchange Rate Mechanism. After this disaster for the Conservatives, Labour moved ahead in the opinion polls, while its leader John Smith's sudden death from a heart attack in May 1994 made way for Tony Blair to lead the party.

The party's weakness and desperation to become a competitive entity once more gave Blair considerable power to lead change, and he carried out the most radical transformation in Labour's whole history.

The hard question was 'How do we get the British people to think that we're competent once again and become viable contenders for power?' Aided by former adman Philip Gould, Blair and his associates started by talking to the public and asking them what they thought and how they felt about their lives, the state of the country and the Labour Party. Gould was portrayed in the media

And So To (More) Politics

as a sinister Svengali who brought the black arts of marketing to politics but all he was doing was elementary qualitative research, of the type that had been used by commercial brands for decades, and indeed by both the Republicans and Democrats in the US.

Like much research, the focus groups confirmed what most people already knew but many Labourites had tried to ignore. Labour had strayed too far from the centre and the major concerns of most of the electorate.

Within a short while, the famous Clause 4 on nationalisation had been dropped from the party's constitution and the term 'socialism' had been removed from the Labour manifesto. Furthermore Labour was rebranded 'New Labour' to emphasise the break from the past and the previously perceived highly left-wing flavour of the party.

The Blair leadership also adopted the 'Third Way' theory produced by the sociologist Anthony Giddens, which aimed at achieving a coherent synthesis of social democratic and market liberalism policies. The importance of this positioning derived less from the ideas themselves than from its clear signal to the centrist middle classes that Labour understood their concerns and values and would not abandon them as in the past.

By understanding the importance of its hard question and finding comprehensive and productive answers, the Labour Party was finally able to gain the public's confidence once more and take advantage of the Conservative Party's weakness. In 1997 it swept to power with a landslide majority of 179, winning further elections in 2001 and 2005.

David Cameron, leader of the Conservative Party since 2005, had to handle a similar hard question in his bid to restore the public's trust in the party and make it electable once more. The Tories had been riven by bitter personal and policy splits ever since Margaret Thatcher was dethroned in 1990. It was only Labour's weakness and its then leader Neil Kinnock's personal unpopularity that allowed John Major to lead the Tories to victory in 1992.

Like Labour before it, the Conservatives moved too far away from the centre. There were deep and public divisions over Thatcher's ousting and also membership of the European Union, despite this being a long way down the list of the public's concerns. For 15 years the party rejected centrist candidates and voted in a succession of old-style right-wing leaders, giving it an increasingly narrow-minded partisan appearance, which enabled political opponents to label it the 'nasty' party. It was perceived as uncaring about the poor and unfortunate, opposed to the welfare state and anti-foreigners.

When it lost in 2005 the Tory Party was destined to be out of power for as long as 13 consecutive years, unthinkable for a party which had ruled for two-thirds of the 20th century. So by electing the young, modern and centrist Cameron, the nearest candidate they had to a Blair clone, the Tories were signalling that they too realised that change was needed.

Cameron's hard question was 'How do we get the British people to believe that we're nice, civilised people again and so become viable contenders for power?'

In contrast to Blair, Cameron implicitly went backwards to redefine the Tory brand. He returned to the core strand of beliefs that had served the Conservatives so well in the previous 100 years: 'one nation conservatism', a famous phrase deriving indirectly from Benjamin Disraeli, the highly successful leader in the 19th century

The basis of one nation conservatism is a belief in social cohesion, and its adherents support social institutions that maintain harmony between different interest groups, classes, and – more recently – different races or religions. These institutions have typically included the welfare state, the BBC, and local government. Cameron emphasised support for the welfare state, in particular the National Health Service, while previous leader Iain Duncan-Smith focused on the poor with a series of well-regarded reports suggesting innovative policies for tackling poverty. And Cameron attempted to keep Europe off the agenda as much as possible.

By 2009 with the Tories enjoying a substantial lead in the polls for

And So To (More) Politics

the first time in many years, it was clear that Cameron had achieved the first stage of his objectives. Although this lead was eroded the following year, as the electorate fretted about entrusting the damaged economy to such a youthful untried group as the leading Tories and Nick Clegg's personal performances sent the Lib Dems soaring in the polls, Cameron held his nerve and refused to fall back on the right-wing policies that some of his supporters demanded. And in the end it was only because he had refashioned the image of the Conservatives that Cameron was able to put together the ground-breaking coalition with the Liberal Democrats after the general election in 2010.

Good cause brands can face similar problems. For example, supporting a humanitarian charity that relieves famine might seem pretty straightforward. But what if the charity starts campaigning for political objectives or seems to be taking sides in a conflict? And how do you keep your issues top of mind when there are so many good causes around? They are all competing for the same humanitarian or campaigning pound. Consumers (because that's what they are) also want to be sure that the organisation is spending its money efficiently and not wasting it on administration overheads and expenses. How can the brand ensure that the public trusts it enough to hand over the cash or, increasingly these days, leave them a legacy?

Take three contrasting charities, Oxfam, the Red Cross and Greenpeace, each with its own distinctive brand and approach to its work and supporters.

Oxfam was originally founded in Oxford in the UK in 1942, one of several committees formed to help the National Relief Committee. The aim was to persuade the British government to allow food through the Allied blockade for the people of Axis-occupied Greece. Oxfam International is now a federation of 14 such organisations across the world. While the initial aim was simply a humanitarian one, to provide food to relieve famine, Oxfam went on to development work, trying to lift communities out of poverty with long-term sustainable solutions and then, more contentiously, lobbying and campaigning at local, national and governmental levels.

Its chosen remit now covers trade, fair trade, education, debt, health, gender equality, conflicts, democracy, human rights and climate change. So it's a highly political organisation, especially as about a quarter of its revenues comes from governments and similar sources. Oxfam's policies and campaigns have brought it into conflict with a range of bodies, from Israel to Starbucks while other NGOs have criticised it for being too close to the UK government under Tony Blair. Clearly its brand has changed through the years as its range of causes has widened to include just about every aspect of life in the developing world.

The Red Cross goes all the way back to the 1850s. Henry Dunant was running the Swiss colony of Setif in Algeria and needed authorisation for a land concession so that he could build a wheat mill. After meeting several bureaucratic obstacles, Dunant decided to go to the man who really called the shots, French emperor Napoleon III. Dunant tracked him to northern Italy where Napoleon was engaged in the battle of Solferino. What suffering Dunant saw there inspired him to set up an organisation that would provide 'care given to the wounded in wartime by zealous, devoted and thoroughly qualified volunteers'.

Since then the well-established and respected charity has by and large managed to maintain its brand values of being impartial, neutral, independent and humanitarian. Of course this is essential since the Red Cross sends its people into extremely dangerous areas of conflict and can only protect them by staying out of campaigning and political lobbying.

Greenpeace, on the other hand, was set up as a radical, overtly campaigning organisation that uses direct protests and other actions to further its cause. Established in 1971 when some activists sent a boat to Alaska to protest at the US testing of nuclear devices, the focus of the organisation later turned from anti-nuclear protest to other environmental issues: whaling, bottom trawling,

And So To (More) Politics

global warming, old growth, nuclear power and genetically modified organisms.

Direct action is the most visible sign of the Greenpeace brand. In addition to conventional environmental organisation methods, such as lobbying businesses and politicians and participating in international conferences, Greenpeace uses direct action to attract attention to particular environmental problems. For example, activists place themselves between the whaler's harpoons and their prey or invade nuclear facilities dressed as barrels of radioactive waste. And to emphasise its radical independent nature, it accepts no donations from governments, political parties or corporations.

Each of these charities will have to work hard to maintain the distinctiveness of its brand and keep it adjusted to the changing nature of the charity marketplace and customers' perceptions. The hard questions they will face will relate to changing views of aid to the developing world, the economic prospects of the developed world and the public's perceptions of what kind of charity is most effective in dealing with these problems.

The BBC, one of the most respected broadcasting organisations in the world has also faced, and continues to face, hard questions forced upon it by a period of immense technological and therefore consumer change and reorientation.

Founded in 1922 by Lord Reith as a public service with the imposing mission statement 'to educate, entertain and inform', the BBC was a pioneering not-for-profit body, funded solely by the universal licence fee and yet supposed to be independent of the government of the day. For decades it towered over the media landscape, a unique institution providing news, factual programming, entertainment and education on first radio and then television. Throughout its life it pioneered technological and broadcasting innovation, launching colour television, Ceefax and Nicam stereo and it appeared to be determined to be in the forefront of broadcasting development in any shape or form.

One Hard Question

It met its first great challenge in 1955 when the commercial broadcaster ITV entered the arena, which soon forced the BBC to become more popular in its content and less like an educational institution giving its audience what it thought was good for it. In the 1960s it adapted to the challenge of the rock and roll pirate radio stations by updating and popularising its radio content and style. By astutely balancing the differing demands of its public service and popular entertainment remits the BBC managed to maintain competitive ratings against both commercial TV (including the introductions of Channel 4 and Channel Five) and also the range of new commercial radio stations.

The most significant development in the industry however was the launch of Rupert Murdoch's Sky TV in 1989, which led the way to an explosion of cable and satellite channels in the UK and changed the way audiences watch TV. Sky challenged the BBC in two ways, first through content as it competed financially to secure the best live sports events that had traditionally fallen into the BBC's lap. By securing the UK Premier League and then a range of rugby, cricket and other leading competitions, Sky attracted prime audiences and also sowed resentment among viewers who expected to see these events free-to-air instead of having to subscribe, or even worse, pay one-off extra charges (as with championship boxing) for the privilege.

Secondly Sky's business model threatened the free-to-air concept that had been the accepted, traditional system for nearly 70 years. Now the media, politicians and the public began to ask why they had to pay for media consumption through what was essentially a universal tax, instead of being able to pick and choose their viewing as they would with virtually any other product or service.

The BBC's hard question was 'How do we maintain our position as the leading brand at the heart of the UK media universe when that universe is expanding so fast and in so many different ways?' With Rupert Murdoch and other economic libertarians lobbying hard to reduce the BBC's power, there was the distinct danger that the BBC might find itself on the way to the type of ghetto occupied by the public broadcasting system in the US.

The BBC's response was to go on the attack and compete in every area possible to demonstrate to the public that they were still getting good value for their licence fees and that it did not need to carry advertising or sponsorship.

Bolstered by the secure funding it had from the licence fee the BBC launched a range of new channels, including BBC News, a 24 hour rolling news channel, BBC Parliament, later followed by BBC Three and BBC Four, and two children's channels, CBBC and CBeebies. It has also launched a whole range of regional, ethnic and local radio stations and has bolstered its educational provision with services aimed at supporting pupils taking the GCSE examinations. It speedily turned itself into the world's leading provider of education and learning for a multi-media environment and it now transmits more general and specialised programming than any other broadcaster.

The BBC also enthusiastically entered the internet age, with its own comprehensive and leading news and current affairs website, backed up by countless websites for its individual TV and radio programmes and differing interest groups. It pioneered digital teletext and launched the interactive red button service where, for example, viewers can pick which Wimbledon tennis match they wish to watch out of several running at the same time.

The BBC then embraced the unique interactive aspects of internet technology by building committed relationships with its audiences. Consumers could now contact their favourite programmes through any number of ways from emails to phone texts. And in response to the video on demand trend, its iPlayer was launched to allow people to watch programmes on their PC up to a week after transmission.

It also worked at building its brand internationally by investing further in its highly respected radio channel, BBC World Service, and with the launch of BBC America and BBC World TV channels.

Further developments included a drive to exploit its archive and commercial portfolio and work harder to supplement the licence fee through programme and publishing sales and commercial joint ventures whose profits are reinvested in the core service.

BBC Worldwide, the Corporation's commercial subsidiary was revamped and energised to build greater revenues from selling BBC magazines, videos, books, audio and visual materials and has regularly generated additional yearly revenues of about £150 million for the BBC. In the UK it launched subscription channels under the UKTV brand in a joint venture with Flextech and other channels with the Discovery Channel.

As part of this sustained commercial campaign, the BBC became the third largest magazine publisher in the UK, which led to attacks from commercial publishers that it was using taxpayers' money to abuse its position and drive commercial publishers out of business.

These criticisms were echoed in the recession of 2008–9 by commercial radio networks and newspaper companies, which pointed out that when everyone else had to cut back in the face of the recession it was time for the BBC to be forced to concentrate on the narrower remit of its public service duties. Other critics suggested that the BBC should introduce charging for its dominating website. Following these criticisms and the austerity measures brought in by the Coalition in 2010, the BBC then responded to the change in public mood, with cuts in its budget and services in return for a guaranteed licence fee for the following few years.

Nevertheless, in overall terms the BBC had managed to deal well with the threats of multi-channel TV, the internet and mobile phone communications. By now audiences could access information and entertainment in a dazzling number of ways in whatever media formats they wished. These included interactive and digital television, electronic programmes guides, phone technology, personal video recorders and the omnipresent internet.

Despite this proliferation of competitive forms of communication

And So To (More) Politics

and entertainment, from Sky Sports to YouTube and iPhone applications, the BBC fought its way through two decades of unprecedented change to remain at the heart of the UK media industry.

While the growth in the number of TV channels and the increased usage of the internet fragmented the audiences for all the main UK channels, the BBC was still achieving an audience share of nearly 40 per cent for its two main channels, BBC One and BBC Two, while the average weekly reach of its website bbc.co.uk was more than 12 million.

And the BBC also managed to retain the approval of the public. In a 2009 poll an overwhelming majority, 77 per cent, thought the BBC was an institution people should be proud of – up from 68 per cent in an equivalent poll carried out five years previously. Similarly, 63 per cent also thought it provided good value for money – up from 59 per cent in 2004. Significantly, the licence fee was backed by 43 per cent, against 24 per cent who thought advertising should foot the bill and 30 per cent who believed people should pay to subscribe if they wanted to see BBC programmes.

Clearly the BBC did successfully answer its hard question. While it may well have to slim down in the future or take a smaller licence fee, it has managed to build a successful platform of digital and interactive channels and services that should enable it to be competitive in the media landscape of the forthcoming decades.

Arguably the most important issue in modern life is trust. People and companies need to persuade others to trust them. This applies just as much in terms of, say, your own credit rating as it does to companies' ability to raise money and ride out difficulties.

These days we don't trust the banks or politicians, or so every bit of research tells us. It's doubtful actually that we ever wholly did (certainly not politicians) but maybe we used to trust them a bit more. And maintaining trust for companies, other institutions and even whole countries is more difficult than ever with a 24/7 news cycle.

Somewhere in the world a metaphorical bomb is going to go off and your reputation is immediately on the line.

This is why so-called reputation management, what we used to call public relations, is so important these days. Unlike most marketing communication activities it's about preparing for the worst rather than trying to build sales and profits.

But persuading people to trust your brand is still the best way to survive this shark-infested global pool.

Apple has overtaken Microsoft (from a very long way back) because of its brilliant products and its reputation for providing the very best technology (at a price) in the best and most attractive guise and, crucially, not hammering buyers with expensive upgrade costs every time it improves them. So, by and large, we trust Apple in a way we don't trust Microsoft and the company has profited accordingly.

So maybe the hardest question of all, but one that all brand owners need to ask themselves, is 'How do we create trust?'

Well you can do it. The most successful supermarket brand in the UK through the recession has been Waitrose, owned by the John Lewis Partnership.

For decades Waitrose was an up-market grocer, appealing to many for the quality and variety of its food but unlikely to be the main shop of the week for most people because of price. But a few years ago it introduced its Essentials brand, essentially food sold at the same kind of price that its rivals offered for their standard products. They, meanwhile, were introducing even cheaper 'value' lines. But these often looked cheap and nasty (and in some cases still do). You felt a bit of a peasant picking one up. Would it poison your family? Waitrose Essentials, on the other hand, looked OK and they still managed to keep most of the quality image Waitrose products had among consumers, even the ones who didn't shop there.

Net result? Waitrose sales have surged through the recession because more people now feel they can shop there. They trust the

And So To (More) Politics

store and they trust Essentials. And it's a lot cooler to walk around with a Waitrose 'bag for life' than with one from Tesco or Asda.

So it can be done.

All that's required is to ask the right hard questions, particularly ones aimed at establishing trust in your brand.

And hope that one of the modern world's unpredictable disasters isn't lurking around the corner.

10

And Then Came the Internet

British scientist Tim Berners-Lee invented the world wide web in 1989 and the means of linking it all together, the internet, arrived a year later.

Some years before that someone asked Chinese premier Zhou Enlai, a rather more cosmopolitan figure than his boss Mao Zedong, what he thought had been the impact of the French Revolution in 1789.

'It's too early to say,' said Zhou.

Now it probably won't take the best part of 200 years to ascertain the impact of the internet but it's safe to say that its scope and importance is still full of surprises and barely glimpsed potential.

It has already revolutionised the world of branding and marketing, in part as a medium of communication, in part as the enabler of huge global brands that nobody envisaged before it got under way. These include the search giants Google and Yahoo and huge online communities such as Facebook, YouTube and Twitter.

It also poses a severe challenge to some of the most famous brands of our time, traditional media owners that are suddenly confronted with not just a rival or rivals but extinction. Nearly all media depend to a degree on advertising as their main source of income. Most, but not all, newspapers and magazines charge a cover price too, but advertising is likely to be the biggest contributor to funds.

Traditional television companies, often termed 'terrestrial,' are wholly dependent on advertising in its various forms to fund programme making, distribution costs and, hopefully, a profit at the end of the day. As such they have seen competitors for advertising

One Hard Question

come and go but the end result has usually been, at worst, a rather smaller slice of a rather larger advertising cake.

But the challenge from the internet is much more fundamental, not so much in terms of display advertising (classified is another story) but from search. This, essentially, is the business of promoting your brand or product on the internet by manoeuvring it to the top of Google pages. So if you're looking for a holiday somewhere or a washing machine you go to Google and see that particular holiday or Whirlpool washing machines at the top of the page. And you may well decide that'll do for you and you need to go no further. It's a throwback to the days when lots of companies were called ABC or Acme, just to appear early on in the telephone directory. Zulu washing machines might not have done as well.

Companies secure these prime Google listings by paying directly for them and by paying agencies to use all sorts of clever devices to trump what their competitors are doing. And the clients can see immediately what they're getting for their money. Our old friend Lord Leverhulme would have been a fan of search.

In recent years search has soared away to propel internet or online advertising to be the single biggest advertising medium in many countries. It's actually debatable whether search should be called advertising at all. It's really direct marketing, albeit through a medium funded by advertising. But it's big and it's not going to go away, not until someone invents a better way of finding information than using Google anyway.

The internet also boasts display and classified advertising. Advertisers usually pay for display advertising on a 'per click' basis, so that has a lot in common with direct marketing too. The weakness of display advertising on the internet is that, although it measures total numbers instantly, it doesn't tell you who's looking at the ads in any useful detail.

It tells you which computer they're using and which search engines they used to find you. But, unless users register, you can't really form a relationship with them. And online sites pull in viewers from all over the place. The *Daily Mail*'s website pulls in many millions of viewers, so-called unique users, a month. But a large proportion of these are in the US, which is not much use to a UK advertiser.

Classified advertising, usually small ads for jobs, cars and property, is a different matter. Classified ads on the internet are much cheaper than ones printed on paper and so they have migrated to the net in droves, threatening publications that depend on them such as local papers and trade magazines. Most such publishers now have their own websites but, because of the very low barriers to entry on the internet, there's much more competition and rates are lower. So the internet is not nearly as profitable for these publishers as paper.

A further worrying factor for traditional media owners is that, while their earth-bound brands may resonate with an audience of a certain age who will then go to their websites, a whole generation of consumers has grown up who have always turned first to the internet. The *New York Times* or the *Daily Mail* is therefore a far smaller presence in their lives.

These, for many media owners, rather grim developments have led some commentators to speculate that the days of traditional media, newspapers, magazines and television are well and truly over. And certainly the search is on for a new business model with some media owners taking the view that the only solution is to persuade online readers and viewers of videos to pay for the privilege.

Others see the future in terms of taking a leaf out of the social networking sites book by, in effect, turning themselves into communities. This would at least produce the benefit of reader registration, making it possible to determine the status of the audience more accurately. Because if search, especially the all-conquering Google, was the first great internet commercial phenomenon, communities constitute the second.

Fashionable communities come and go with bewildering speed. It's not so long ago that Friends Reunited was taking the UK by storm,

One Hard Question

prompting ITV to pay around £200m to acquire it as the cornerstone of its online strategy. A few years later it was sold for barely a tenth of that price as other communities like Facebook and Twitter overtook it.

Rupert Murdoch's News Corporation paid over $500m for MySpace with similar hopes to ITV's for Friends Reunited. MySpace too has now been overtaken by a fickle young audience's preference for other sites, and possible aversion to one owned by News Corp., although it's still in there fighting.

The one hard question that brand owners are asking themselves in this brave new world is, 'where's my place in it?'

Because, although Facebook and Twitter are commercial entities, ultimately all the owners really do is provide server capacity because the content is created by users.

It's a similar story in the so-called blogosphere in which millions of writers across the world offer their thoughts, opinions and prejudices freely to readers across the world. Most blogs are happy to accept ads, many of which are provided by the ever-useful Google's AdSense, but, although they take away readers from mainstream media's online content, few of them are big enough in themselves to take their place.

Furthermore the members of online communities and the readers of millions of blogs are not, by and large, especially receptive to the offerings of advertisers. One of the things they like about the internet is that it isn't always trying to sell them something, unlike mainstream media.

The exception to this are 'gadget' blogs like www.boingboing.com that garner huge audiences online who are relatively happy to click on ads for the gadgets they've read about. So technology advertisers at least are happy with the encroachments of the internet. Techie fans, of course, are genuinely interested in the latest offering from technology companies, a happy co-incidence of editorial and advertising. Put another way, they create their own community.

It's not quite the same if you're trying to sell soap or breakfast cereal or beer or any of the other mainstays of advertising in the 20th century to an online audience. But that hasn't stopped these brand owners trying.

Coca-Cola and Starbucks are just two of the brands trying to garner their own supporters on Facebook. In 2009 both boasted over three million users of the site signed up to specific Coke and Starbucks 'friends' groups. Other major marketers such as P&G and Unilever are exploring the same route.

Three million, especially for a supposedly unloved brand like Starbucks, sounds a lot but in the context of audiences heading for a billion it's not that significant, statistically anyway.

The other huge global internet community is YouTube, now owned by Google. In Chapter 6 we discussed the way some advertisers would produce extremely lavish commercials in the hope that YouTube users would take to it and, in effect, provide the media exposure for nothing. Many advertisers now make 'viral' films, often weird and whacky vignettes featuring their brand somewhere or other with the same intention in mind. Now there are opportunities for advertisers on a sponsored part of YouTube as the company tries to build its own revenues.

But this doesn't really answer the brand owner's one hard question, 'Where's my place in this ever-shifting world?'

Just as the likes of MySpace and Bebo took over from Friends Reunited and then, in turn, were supplanted by Facebook and Twitter in a few short years, one receives the strong impression that brand owners are chasing consumers around the ether rather than being able to make a measured pitch to them.

With a newspaper or magazine or commercial TV channel you know where the audience is, more or less who they are and what they like and dislike. Far too often on the internet brand owner efforts are like the uncle who embarrasses you at a wedding by trying to dance like the youngsters. The audience just turns the other way.

Some communication channels remain much as they were of

One Hard Question

course – packaging and point of sale to name two. Online shopping has affected even these, with most big retailers now offering home deliveries for internet orders and many people, for bigger ticket items anyway, window shopping for products before returning to their screens and finding the cheapest offer online. Packaging and point of sale are clearly less effective (and in many cases wholly irrelevant) on the internet.

But the vast majority of shoppers still shop in shops, for everyday items anyway, and so the importance of packaging and point of sale has, if anything, increased relative to other communications options. Packaging has certainly developed a much more strident tone of voice in recent years as brand owners have striven to make their expensive supermarket space work harder. They then have to bite their lips as the supermarkets copy the packaging for their own brands.

And it's fair to say that retailers have adapted to the online world more readily than most manufacturers. This includes a large number of online-only retailers of whom two of the most noted are Amazon, which began as an online bookseller and now sells a huge range of products, and iTunes, Apple's phenomenally successful download music service.

Apple has also turned its iPhone into a successful online retail business by launching a vast number of applications or 'apps', extra services submitted by other developers with whom it shares the revenues.

Then, of course, there is Ebay, the online auction service, which now acts as a host for a large number of other businesses which use its infrastructure to run their own smaller but, in many cases, still substantial businesses.

Online businesses rise (and often fall) very swiftly indeed and an interesting example is the *Huffington Post*, perhaps the first serious online challenger to established traditional media brand owners. The *HuffPost* was founded in 2005 as a news and comment aggregator by socialite author and columnist Arianna Huffington and journalists Kenneth Lederer and Jonah Peretti in New York.

News aggregators, of which Google News is the biggest and best known, hoover up relevant content from the internet (much of provided by traditional media owners) and collect it all in one place.

This clearly irks the traditional media owners but they are faced with a conundrum: withdraw their content from Google News and others and readers will just get it somewhere else. And Google News drives huge amounts of traffic to their sites so they need it to keep their numbers up.

The *HuffPost* majors more on comment than news, attracting bloggers from Barack Obama and Hillary Clinton to Nora Ephron, Robert Redford and the late Edward Kennedy. Acting as a counterpoint to the many right-wing blogs that once dominated the blogosphere, like the *Drudge Report*, it attracts a wide range of liberal commentators and readers, who also supply it with more than a million comments each month.

It overtook the celebrated *Washington Post* in terms of monthly traffic and was the first online only journalistic product to suggest that the internet can support 'proper' journalism (it has a staff of 60 including its own columnists) through attracting advertising.

Investors seem to think so anyway. Although it had so far not made a profit, it was snapped up for $315 million in 2011 by AOL, which, after its disastrous merger with Time Warner, was looking for ways to prevent itself dropping out of the internet's premier league.

Similarly another entry to the upper reaches of the blogosphere set up by former *Vanity Fair* editor Tina Brown, the *Daily Beast*, named after the fictional newspaper in Evelyn Waugh's Fleet Street satire *Scoop*, merged in 2010 with *Newsweek*, another traditional media owner casting around for a strategy to combat eroding readerships and revenues.

Whether either of these ventures can make a profit out of offering free content remains to be seen. Or will the Murdoch strategy of

One Hard Question

charging for general news and feature comment prove to be the right option?

In the UK maverick publisher Felix Dennis offers his *First Post*, a similar product which the irrepressible Dennis claims does make a profit although it hardly enjoys the same influence as the *HuffPost* and the *Daily Beast*.

The *HuffPost* averages over 22 million unique users a month although this is not huge by internet standards, British papers like the *Guardian*, *The Times* and the *Telegraph* being in the same area.

Such is the number of people swirling around the internet that you really need even more than this to generate big advertising revenues, which is why aggregation is the current buzz word. This simply means collecting a number of websites together and selling advertising packages across them that can target hundreds of millions of users. Ultimately these numbers should be unarguable from the point of view of an advertiser or a brand owner. The problem they still have, and the one hard question they still need to answer, is 'How do I connect with them?'

In part this is a creative problem. Brand advertising on the internet is still a work in progress, to put it politely. While geeks and nerds (we paraphrase somewhat) will happily click away on any gadget ad that looks interesting, people interested in other products by and large will not. Nor are the ad spaces available on most websites particularly conducive to creative impact.

Video, of course, provides another important advertising option but there are numerous other free videos on the internet which are likely to appear more interesting to a casual viewer than an ad. Most people skip commercials if they get the opportunity.

But to find the real answer it's possible we need to refer all the way back to Chapter 2 and Procter & Gamble's Neil Hosler McElroy who, you may recall, more or less invented the brand management system. This entailed running each brand as a business with its own management team devoted to building share, sales and profit for

And Then Came the Internet

that particular brand, in McElroy's case Camay soap. The chosen means was advertising, press, posters and radio in those days and later commercial television. This ensured distribution in the shops and a large potential market willing to try your product. And this is still the way things work today.

But is it enough when consumers are advertising savvy, scattered across a bewildering array of media and likely to do a part of their shopping at least remotely, via the internet?

Many people today say that marketing is largely about setting budgets. How much do we spend on TV and press, how much on point of sale and retail promotions and how much on that interloper the internet? Uncertainty reigns.

A consequence of this is that, with a few brave exceptions, most companies are only too eager to slash advertising and marketing budgets. This nearly always happens when times get tough even though there is a basketful of research evidence showing that companies who sustain their spend through recessions emerge stronger on the other side. The mighty Unilever, P&G's biggest rival, increased its marketing spend substantially through the recession of 2008–9 and increased both share and profits. P&G, by contrast, cut back. This was regarded as an almighty gamble by Unilever's new CEO Paul Polman but allied to a programme of cost cuts elsewhere in the business it paid off.

But how can companies ensure they make the right call more often?

The key, as McElroy identified, is to put the brand at the heart of every activity. The trouble is that today's big brands, however trusted by consumers they may be, are in a permanent state of flux and much of this can be laid at the door of the internet.

'Word of mouth', what consumers think and say about brands, has always been the most powerful communications medium but brand owners have been able to manipulate it to significant degree. If you broadcast enough commercials showing fictional consumers praising your product and spent enough to ensure you gained prominent display positions in supermarkets, you could more or less guarantee an enduring grocery brand.

To an extent the same was true of bigger ticket items like electrical goods or even cars. Image in these markets was all and clever advertising and promotion was the principal means of creating it.

This led to the era of mighty advertising agencies who nestled at the right hand of company bosses and turned into big businesses themselves by following their clients, mainly from the US, around the world. McCann-Erickson, part of the Interpublic Group and the biggest single agency network in the world, grew by its devotion, mostly reciprocated, to the likes of Coca-Cola, Nestlé and the Exxon oil company. Wherever Coke or Exxon was, so was McCanns. The same is true of British-owned WPP whose US-based agency networks Ogilvy and Mather and JWT grew alongside clients such as Unilever and Ford. When WPP bought another network, Grey, it acquired a large slice of P&G business as well as drugs giant SmithKline Beecham.

A consequence of this was that the client's main marketing adviser would usually, in response to a business problem, recommend advertising as the solution, although these agency networks also offered public relations and store marketing services among others.

The first hole to be blown in these agency monoliths was the explosive growth of independent media agencies, which would often take a different view to the creative agency. But with the exception of the publicly quoted Carat agency all the big media agencies are now owned by the agency supergroups.

The second, and much more significant, explosion, was the internet.

The internet isn't just another medium, it's a whole different way of doing things and it empowers consumers in a way that wasn't possible before. It's now possible for anyone with a computer to influence events worldwide, in business just as much as politics or entertainment, if they attract enough followers.

So an individual blogger can be just as influential as the *New York Times*. Or, if your brand of toothpaste has been criticised on Facebook and sufficient other users have had the same unhappy experience, no amount of paid-for advertising and marketing can undo the effect.

Brand owners, as we noted earlier, have entered the lists to try to build their own groups of supporters on social network sites. Many brand owners enlist prominent bloggers or even create their own groups to try to garner supporters on the internet. Oil giant Exxon has been accused of so doing in the US to counter the climate change lobby.

But even if you come clean about what you're doing, which most companies now do, such internet recommendation will be regarded as tainted by a large part of the online community. And this now constitutes billions of people everywhere.

So the old linear brand management way of trying to manage your commercial fortunes, basically by allocating marketing spend to various priorities, is arguably no longer appropriate when your reputation is being shredded on an hourly basis.

Politicians have been quick to pick up on this. One of the reasons for Barack Obama's in many ways incredible victory in the US Presidential election of 2008 was his campaign team's mastery of internet strategy. This had hitherto been the preserve of his Republican opponents who had benefited from right-wing bloggers rubbishing Democrats of all hues throughout the George Bush era.

TV ads no doubt played their part in the outcome in 2008 as obviously did televised debates between Obama and opponent John McCain and reporting and comment in the newspapers and on radio and TV.

But the internet was doubly important. It played host to a constant debate among Americans about the rights and wrongs of the candidates, with the Democrats finally marshalling their own online warriors. And it was also the medium through which Obama raised

One Hard Question

millions of dollars in small campaign donations, thereby helping to nullify the advantage of big business dollars for the Republicans.

Brands too now have to fight their corner in this potent and often unruly medium. And, as we mentioned before, straightforward advertising on the internet is not as potent as one would expect, even given the huge numbers of people who can be reached.

Yet it's also true that no one medium ever completely displaces another. There will always be newspapers (although a number of smaller ones are already switching to online only) and commercial TV (although you may actually watch it via an internet feed).

Pity the poor brand manager who has to try to make sense of this. For many companies the solution has been to deploy an online advertising agency to add to the long list of advertising, media, packaging, design, sales promotion and PR agencies they already have. Which just means one more hungry piglet snuffling away at the trough of the increasingly stretched marketing budget.

It seems inevitable that brand owners will need to move to a more flexible system to reflect an increasingly flexible and in many ways more short-term commercial environment. The task will be to try to influence the conversations people are having about their brands (managing them is probably too much to expect). So what people think about your call centre, how you perform on price comparison websites and what the bloggers think of you will be arguably more important than advertising or packaging.

People with the same skills as Barack Obama's campaign team will be needed to steer brands through these turbulent waters. And the people trying to co-ordinate this for the brand owner may still be called brand managers and marketing managers and directors (or even chief marketing officers as they call the top bananas in the US these days) but they'll really be the equivalent of a 'brand community manager', someone who tries to influence consumers wherever they meet the brand. It is indeed a daunting job description and perhaps the first quality required is the knowledge that you can't hope to do everything or win every time. Just how much can a company influence a world where the consumer is now quite definitely, and probably permanently, on top?

This is one hard question that very few companies, so far, have found an answer to.

11
Creatively Intelligent or Intelligently Creative

Is there a difference?

Yes, in so far as brand owners and their agencies need to be creative in their thinking and intelligent about the creative approach and solutions they adopt.

Very often this means *not* rushing to the obvious solution to a problem, as this may mean that all they are doing is repeating the mistakes of the past. So more and better advertising or more attractive packaging may not produce the results expected because the starting point is wrong.

So where do we start from?

We've tried to show in this book how companies and brands prospered by asking One Hard Question and pointed out how, along the route, this may have occurred from accident or happenstance. So how can you instil this as a deliberate business practice?

Arguably what makes a hard question difficult to answer is not revealed by the solution you arrive at. Many marketing solutions appear deceptively simple. How on earth did it cost so much time and money to get there, people ask themselves.

This is because the hard part is being able to ask the right question in the first place and, crucially, ask that hard question in such a way that it helps to stimulate an engaging and persuasive solution.

So the difficulty comes in developing the strategic insight to be able to identify the right question (being creatively intelligent) and possessing the insight to ask it in the right way (being intelligently creative).

But when we're faced with a problem our natural inclination is to jump straight to a solution. Answers, of course, are the ultimate objective but the best way to get there is to invest time and money in getting the question right first.

Most of our clients accept this because it's really common sense. But the trouble in business is that you are dealing with internal structures which may be inimical to such an approach and external factors that force your hand to rapid action.

And this is even before you've had time to think about the consumer, the person who ultimately decides if your business succeeds or fails.

Most businesses are solution-driven of course, because ultimately they need to produce the financial results to satisfy the owners (shareholders), bankers and others like analysts who influence the perception of the company in the marketplace.

Most really big companies, even privately owned ones, report their results quarterly these days, which is a highly unforgiving environment. And quoted companies are measured daily by the performance of the share price, which is even more testing. Neither of these disciplines is conducive to creative intelligence.

The increased speed and complexity of change means that often companies feel powerless. They know that change is happening all around them but can't find even a starting point to help them grapple with it. When they try to analyse the problem and come up with fresh ideas they end up going round in circles. Add to that the way in which today's executives have all their time cut out attending to the constant stream of daily activity necessary just to keep their brands functioning in some sort of reasonable way. It's no wonder that companies get locked into the status quo.

The problem is that brands don't just travel along as if they're on the motorway. Their journeys can be much more like a yomp across uncharted territory, with plenty of pitfalls and ambushes along the way.

And consumers have so much more power these days. The

internet has provided the public with an immense amount of choice and research opportunities plus the ability to communicate their experiences and feelings about a brand across the world in a matter of seconds. The court of consumer opinion never shuts and brings a constant stream of judgements, which means brands and their owners stand trial every day.

What's needed is a different way of thinking and looking at brands and the markets they're in. People with different skills, ideas and experience of a wide range of brands and markets, who bring a restless curiosity to whatever they look at. By scrutinising the company and the world it operates in from the outside and focusing for weeks on the problems, we can spotlight the key issues, identify the hard question and, just as important, use our creative skills to ask it in the right way.

The aim is to reach a credible, relevant and differentiated brand positioning that appeals to a worthwhile target market. And as many of the examples in this book demonstrate, these highly valuable brand positionings can be arrived at through many different and – some might say – eccentric methods. But most of them involve looking at the brand and the market in a different way.

Great insights tend to come from gaining a deeper understanding of the target audience – or a potential target audience – than the brand has previously demonstrated. Or recognising the key ways in which the competition or the market's aspirations have changed. Or seeing how a basic product or technology can be turned into a brand that provides a completely new benefit, function or status or style, which often the target audience had no idea that they needed or desired.

Look at the way Apple took some standard hardware and memory devices and turned this into a powerful and stylish way to store a whole music collection that the consumer could access 24/7 wherever they were.

Yet you don't have to invent a whole new industry, downloads, as Apple did. In many established, mature markets, the ground rules are established and the capacity for major technological or product advantage are limited. In these cases, a small tweak of the visuals or a retargeting of the consumer can make an immense difference. It's all a question of identifying the key issue and not bringing a ready-made solution or favourite technique to the problem before it's been analysed and understood.

My company, 1HQ, is a brand agency and we are brought in to help companies when they have a problem or they want to do something differently or, in rare cases, try something completely new.

Mostly companies approach us about brands which require revitalising or, less often, revolutionising. It's very rare to be given a blank sheet of paper and be asked to take the company in a completely different direction or invent a completely new brand although it does happen.

Usually, particularly with very large companies and brands, it's a case of tweaking the brand so it performs better. This may be needed because sales are stagnant or falling, the brand is struggling to gain or maintain distribution in major retailers or the competition appears to have moved the game on a bit and our client wants to catch up.

In the not-so-old days one would have gone straight to research to try to find out what consumers thought about the brand and the competition. This may have been quantitative research, where you ask a large number of consumers some pretty straightforward questions, or qualitative, where you take a small group of people and quiz them at length. This still sometimes happens, of course, but in many cases we find that the company has all the raw data it needs. On many occasions we find it has so much data that it doesn't know what to do with it all.

The answer usually lies closer to home.

This doesn't mean that the company is necessarily doing something wrong, at least in its own terms. The management may be committed and capable with a terrific track record in managing its brands. But something is still going wrong and very often that's to do with external change.

Consumers these days have more buying options than ever before and they are much more knowledgeable about the brands they are offered. They are also much harder to please. Take food products. It's not that long ago that the description 'convenience' food was seen as an unalloyed benefit, whether it was ready-sliced bread or meat chunks in a can. It made food assembly easier and saved you time if not necessarily money. Now the phrase is hardly used but the successors to convenience foods, ready meals, are under ferocious fire from many quarters over their high levels of salt and other additives. Even people who buy them are uneasily aware of these issues.

Factory-produced cakes and biscuits are another product category to come under pressure. People now doubt that they can be good for you if they come off a production line and are packaged in such a way that they are clearly supposed to last for a long time. To make life even harder they are struggling to gain any selling space at all in big supermarkets, where they are positioned next to the clearly fresh and very cheap breads and cakes pouring out of the in-store bakery. So they're suffering from two significant recent changes: the rise in consumer concerns over artificial this and that and the remorseless rise of the in-store bakery.

These are fearsome challenges if you're in the cake business and unlikely to be addressed successfully by a new pack design or a big burst of advertising, assuming that these struggling brands can afford to spend the money.

Even famous brands have to find a new place in today's commercial world. Earlier in the book we described briefly how Heinz Tomato Ketchup, one of the most famous brands ever, was fighting to dispel the (erroneous) impression that it was another processed food. This probably arose because the brand had been around for such a long time. Aren't all these old food brands full of stuff that we don't trust

One Hard Question

any more?

But Heinz Tomato Ketchup wasn't. So we addressed the problem with a new label that said 'grown not made'. Which is nothing more than the truth. We also changed the label to feature a tomato rather than the gherkin which had mysteriously adorned it for a hundred-odd years.

And why did we find this solution? Because, I believe, we asked the right question. This was, 'How can we reassure consumers that Heinz is a healthy, natural product?'

We could have asked lots of other questions such as, 'How do we stay ahead of the competition?' But this wouldn't have been sensible because Heinz Tomato Ketchup doesn't really have any competition. Lapsed Heinz consumers would simply have stopped buying ketchup.

There were two other aspects of Heinz Tomato Ketchup that we felt we needed to deal with even though, on most counts, they would be seen as clear strengths.

One was that kids love it. All fine and dandy but many parents these days feel that anything their kids like is bound to be full of sugar and salt and all sorts of other nasties. So one of the brand's greatest strengths was in fact a disadvantage with a growing number of consumers.

The other, which links in with the first, is the company the brand sometimes kept. Heinz Tomato Ketchup is the almost inevitable accompaniment to burgers and other fast food. Heinz could argue that it's just about the healthiest ingredient in such a meal but that doesn't help with parents who are trying to wean their offspring off such delights. The burger connection was decidedly not helping at the supermarket or grocery store point of sale.

This, of course, is where most such purchasing decisions are made so a timely reminder of Heinz Tomato Ketchup's green credentials, via a green label, was, in our view a much better way to get the message across than, say, a big advertising campaign.

Back at the bakery counter, Kingsmill bread recognised that an increasing number of people, often living on their own, didn't need or want the traditional full-sized loaf, as they found themselves throwing half of it away at the end of the week. But people were remarkably unenthusiastic about the half sizes on offer even though they clearly matched a consumer need. Men were particularly unsatisfied.

We looked at the problem, asking why people were being so defiantly illogical about bread, and discovered that while they were fine about half-size loaves they didn't like wimpy, three quarters-sized bread slices. The smaller size slices appearing in smaller-sized loaves just didn't seem like proper bread to our macho market. So we persuaded Kingsmill to try the same-sized bread, just fewer slices. And sales increased markedly.

'A statement of the bleedin' obvious', you might say, but it wasn't so obvious at the time. We needed to ask some hard questions of consumers and our own brand expectations to come up with a deceptively simple answer.

But why do these great big companies, who surely understand the theory and practice of branding and marketing, need brand agencies and advertising agencies and design agencies to help them solve their problems – ask the hard questions that they must surely be aware of themselves?

Partly it's because the people who work in them are too close to the problems to see them clearly, partly it's because big companies are increasingly process driven. In the race to become leaner and more efficient they've stripped out time to think. Partly it's because people like us bring the experience of working on many brands to the problems faced by just one.

Of course you can argue the merits of brand agencies against ad agencies or any other kind of agency, and we do. Our point is that we are 'media neutral' in terms of the solutions we recommend whereas an ad or design agency is most likely to recommend advertising or new packaging as the solution to brand problems.

In fact design is a big part of 1HQ's offer and was used to great effect on behalf of Heinz and Kingsmill in the examples we've just given. But we didn't start from the point that a new pack was needed.

That's where we stand and I hope this book helps brand owners and their agencies understand a bit more about how brands developed and the key questions (and answers) that played a pivotal role in the process.

And in this spirit of selfless generosity we offer all the brand owners who, for some reason, are not our clients, and even their agencies, the following 1HQ Ten Top Tips on Brand Strategy. They're not the whole answer but we hope that they will shed a little light.

Brand Strategy: 1HQ's Ten Top Tips

1. Your brands are more than logos and products.
They are the embodiment of your business among its customers and the focal point around which their opinions form. Think of them as living things that need constant nurturing to ensure healthy growth.

The Disney brand is far more recognisable than its logo. It has built a reputation for making 'dreams come true' for the audience. Disney is known globally as a family-orientated company based on good wholesome values. This is the pinnacle the brand has evolved to.

2. Be crystal clear who your consumer or customer is and what you do for them more effectively than anyone else.
These two things make for the essential promise of your brand; understand it, and stick to it.

The Mini is a great example of this. Through decades (and changes in ownership) it has stayed in touch with its urban, forward-thinking audience and catered for their desire to have some fun when they drive.

John Lewis drove its brand forward by staying loyal to its customer base with its 'never knowingly undersold' position, promising to match its competitors on price. John Lewis used this motto for 82 years, resulting in a reputation for caring about customers.

Carlsberg clearly targets young to middle-aged men with its long-running 'probably the best lager in the world' campaign, proclaiming that 'if Carlsberg did goal celebrations they'd probably be the best goal celebration in the world', and numerous other variations. Carlsberg is one of the nation's biggest-selling lagers amongst its target audience. It doesn't try to be something it's not. It knows what it is and what its customers want.

3. Identify the most effective way to communicate this promise.
Advertising is one way but there are many others.

If budgets are tight, be focused in your approach and creative in your thinking. Smart PR can be a cost-effective way to get exposure and to generate word of mouth amongst consumers.

Just ask the founders of Innocent. The smoothies company used minimal advertising at the outset, adhering to the philosophy that, if you build a good brand, customers will come. It used off-the-wall ideas in the early years, such as sending a minibus round London offering people free lifts. This was a cost-effective way of getting their product recognised. Its tongue-in-cheek advice on the bottles has helped the brand keep in touch with customers and have some fun along the way.

4. Don't just say what you do – do what you say.
Socrates said: 'The way to gain a good reputation is to endeavour to be what you desire to appear.' These days, it's never been more important to walk the walk, as well as talk the talk.

Nike is the most obvious example with its constant commitment to creating the best in sporting goods. The world's biggest trainer manufacturer has given customers what they want by customising its products.

One Hard Question

5. Wherever possible, take a distinctive stance in your market.
Occupying the middle ground only leaves you open to attack from more directions.

Dove went down a 'Real Beauty' route that clearly differentiated it in specific markets and built a billion-dollar brand. The challenge now is how to communicate the message in local cultures. Dove's more realistic attitude towards its products has separated it from other beauty manufacturers, all of whom seem to assume that their customers look like fashion models. This is why Dove has managed to stand out as a leader in this market and develop a brand with a reputation for excellence.

6. Never stop expanding your knowledge of your customer – but don't expect answers from them, only clues.
More and more we find ourselves undertaking 'real world' or ethnographic research where we learn by observing consumers as they go about their daily lives, rather than by asking them for their opinions in focus groups.

Nestlé's recent launch of its new confectionary product Randoms is an example of how 1HQ helped to build a brand around the culture of its target audience rather than just listening to what the audience says. This is an excellent way of relating your product to your audience.

7. Remember there will always be an emotional and sometimes irrational component in a customer's relationship with your brand.
It can't always be controlled but if it's understood it can be influenced.

Consumers have now become communicators and, with multiple channels of communication available to them, have the power to influence brands both positively and negatively.

Toyota is an example of how a brand's equity can appear to be destroyed overnight. Crisis management there has been rightly criticised but the company is fighting back, often via its own internet channels such as one on Twitter aggregator Tweetmeme.

So even if a brand is under ferocious scrutiny it does not mean it's a complete write-off.

Everyone remembers the Tylenol fiasco, where people died from its medicines being laced with cyanide, nearly sparking the end of the company. The introduction of tamper-proof bottles restored faith in the company and actually saw sales revenue rise again.

8. Change is inevitable if your brand is to stay contemporary and relevant but don't be tempted to abandon founding principles in favour of the latest trend.

1HQ recently gave McDougalls flour a new identity and packaging – but the brief focused on the same core promise that has been at the heart of the brand since it first appeared in 1864: inspiring and helping people to experience the pleasure of home baking. And the next generation of consumers have been stimulated in a new way.

Brands also need to work out how to engage with the target consumer and refresh their appetite for entertainment. McDonald's, for example, continues to confound its critics amid the highly competitive fast food market. It now emphasises a localised experience with the best possible ingredients. The company has embraced the notion of healthier eating with open arms. The introduction of salads and fruit pouches for kids has helped McDonald's to continue to flourish in today's more health-conscious world.

9. After the deepest recession of modern times, trust is in short supply.

Brands with authenticity, responsibility and integrity will prosper.

Marks & Spencer might be perceived as conservative but it still holds a special place in our hearts. Rolls-Royce has built up a trustworthy brand over the years that is known for its status, reliability and innovation and has continued to excel over the years despite the ownership changing. Financial institutions on the other hand will have to dig deep. A behaviour shift is essential to restore consumer confidence in a sector where it has been shattered.

10. **When times are tough and budgets tight, focus is essential.**
Often we spend too much time generating answers and not enough ensuring we've got the right question.

What's the One Hard Question your brand is facing this year?

12
There Are More Questions than Answers

But we still need answers!

1HQ is a brand consultancy and we help our clients find the best communications solutions to their problems.

As we've explained, this means asking a number of hard questions, of which there are an infinite number. So how do we find the right ones to ask and then provide answers to them that are accurate, practical and affordable? The key is to start from the right place.

All the examples in this book of brands – companies, even politicians and rulers – that have found the answer to their problems have, knowingly or not, provided solutions which were particular to their times. The questions they asked and the answers they found were rooted in the culture that surrounded them and which they succeeded in influencing. They might not have known it at the time, of course. Henry Vlll wanted a divorce; he didn't (at the outset) want to ditch Roman Catholicism and become a Protestant. Mr Procter and Mr Gamble just wanted to sell more candles and soap. They certainly didn't see their successors inventing the brand management system, inventing the 'soap opera' (there wasn't any radio at the time) or creating the biggest household products company in the world.

To take a more recent example, Nintendo didn't envisage itself being hailed by non-gamers as a key factor in efforts to persuade couch potatoes off their couch and into action when it launched the Wii games console. It just wanted to compete with Sony and Microsoft. But now we read that it's in the front line of the fight against juvenile obesity because you move around when you're playing it.

So the first thing any company needs to do before taking an important marketing decision is to carry out a cultural audit. But what does this mean and how do we do it?

Well it means placing the company's ambitions not just in today's context but in the context of things as they are likely to develop. For a car manufacturer, for example, this currently means making a very large bet on the likely appeal of alternatives to petrol and diesel. We all know that petrol prices are going through the roof and that therefore hybrid and electric cars are very likely the transportation devices of the future (to a large degree hybrid cars already are). But is it worth going the extra mile and going electric?

Two factors affect this. One is the price of petrol and diesel. But what happens if the oil producers bring down their prices as they see the car market slipping away from them? That's the rational conundrum. But there's another. Have consumers reached the stage when they feel (or enough of them feel) that they want to power their cars with something other than refined oil? Regardless, to a degree, of cost.

As Jeremy Bullmore, one-time chairman and creative director of J. Walter Thompson, sagely observed, consumers buy the answer to their needs, not the product. And needs are emotional as well as rational. If those needs include an alternative to horrible gasoline then electric cars may well be the future, regardless of the cost of oil.

This is a matter of culture. Culture can be defined as the outlook, attitudes, values, goals and practices shared by a society. These are passed on from one generation to the next but clearly they change. And the way we buy products and services, and which products and services we buy, changes with them.

So the hard questions we ask and the solutions we seek have to be rooted in an understanding of culture and what is likely to happen to it. We use a number of tools to try to understand this culture and how consumers relate to it. This relationship is absolutely key because people in a given society clearly aren't all the same although they may share, broadly, the same culture.

The tool of choice at the moment is semiotics. 'Semiotics is concerned with everything that can be taken as a sign' (Umberto Eco, A *Theory of Semiotics*,1976). Although closely related to the field of linguistics, semiotics involves the study not only of what we refer to as 'signs' in everyday speech, but of anything which 'stands for' something else. In a semiotic sense, signs take the form of words, images, sounds, gestures and objects.

Semiotics is often divided into three branches:

- *Semantics:* the relationship of signs to what they stand for – their meaning
- *Syntactics:* the formal or structural relations between signs
- *Pragmatics:* the relation of signs to the people who use them/ see them.

Semantics and pragmatics concern us most here. Communication is about signs. When we're devising a new product or advising a company to travel in a certain direction or even designing a new soap powder pack, we need to know what the signs we use (and they might be words or a visual or both) mean to people. And that's semantics.

Pragmatics are the tricky bit: the relationship between signs and the effects signs have on the people who use them. Choose the right signs and people will try your product or service. Get it wrong and they won't, or they will do so only reluctantly or at the cost of an expensive bribe such as an unfeasibly low price. Always bearing in mind that, as Jeremy Bullmore said, people are looking for an answer to their needs (which may not be rational) rather than a better product.

In short (and it's difficult to be short about this) semiotics helps us to get under the skin of commercial issues by revealing *why* people do things. It doesn't tell us everything but it provides some vital and logically verifiable insights into why certain combinations of signs (words, images, music, colour, etc.) work more effectively than others. And if this all sounds a bit sinister it isn't. You can't manipulate people with semiotics, just understand why they do the things they do and like the things they like. It's an analytical tool that explains the culture you need to work with.

The process we therefore adopt when a product or brand comes into the 1HQ A&E department or maternity ward follows five steps:

1. Cultural audit (which is where semiotics comes in)
2. Competitive analysis
3. Strategy development
4. Positioning analysis
5. Platform and creative concept development

What's interesting about this is that the creative concept development (although by no means least in importance) comes last. Get any one of the first four things wrong, fail to ask the One Hard Question, and all the creativity in the world won't help very much.

So there you are. We hope all this has been useful, whether you agree with us or not. And if you don't, please let us know.

The most important thing of all is that we all keep learning.

Index

1HQ 10, 20, 140, 149, 152

Abbott, David 67
Aesop 56
Allen Brady and Marsh 48
Allen, Rod 48
Amazon 128
Apple 18-19, 92, 93, 94-5, 120, 130
Apple Macintosh 92, 93
Ariel 31
Asda 67-8, 70-1
ATV 88

Ballbarrow 56-7
Bass, Saul 47
Baugur 106-07
Bayliss, Trevor 13
BBC 15, 90, 115-16, 117-19
Beckham, David 15
Beecham, Sinclair 79, 80
Bell, Tim 100, 102
Ben and Jerry's 21, 22
Benson & Hedges 45
Berkshire Hathaway 20
Bernback, Bill 46
Berners-Lee, Tim 123
Betfair 24
Black, Andrew 24
Black, Conrad 29
Blair, Tony 110
Bloomingdales 61
BMW 73

Bridgepoint 22
British Gas 89
British Rail 48, 89
British Telecom 89
Brown, Tina 129
BSkyB *see* Sky
Buffett, Warren 20, 27-8
Bullmore, Jeremy 149

Cadbury 21, 28, 64, 72
Callaghan, James 99, 100
Camay 30-1, 32, 42, 44, 45, 131
Cameron, David 111-13
Cannes Golden Lions 33
Capital 89
Carat 132
Carlsberg 145
Carphone Warehouse 76-8
Carrefour 69
CDP see Collett Dickenson Pearce
Central Office of Information 89
Central TV 88
Chance, David 15
Channel 4 15, 89
Chariots of Fire 45
Chiat Day 93
Chisholm, Sam 15
Chrysler 104
Cillit Bang 65
Cinzano 94
Clairol 33
Clow, Lee 93

153

Coca-Cola 19-20, 21, 21-8, 37, 127, 132
Cohen, Jack 62
Colgate-Palmolive 31
Collett Dickensen Pearce 49, 45
Collins, Joan 94
Colman Prentis and Varley 99
comparethemarket.com 73
Conran, Terence 47
Conservative Party 109-10, 111-13
Crispin Porter 94
Cullen, Michael 61

Daily Beast 129
Daily Mail 125
Daily Telegraph 28-9
Dairylea 27
Davies, George 71
Dennis, Felix 130
Diageo 41
Disney 144
Domestos 65
Dove 27, 98, 146
Doyle Dane Bernbach 46
Dunstone, Charles 76-7, 78
Dyke, Greg 90
Dylan, Bob 39, 42
Dyson, James 13, 56-8

Ebay 128
Eco, Umberto *A Theory of Semiotics* 149
Eisenhower, Dwight 35-6
Elizabeth I 53, 54
Energizer Holdings 65
Exxon 132, 133

Facebook 126, 127, 133
Fairy Liquid 48
FedEx 82-3
First Direct 73-6
First Division 15
First Post 130

Fisherman's Friend 28
Fitch, Rodney 47
Florence and Fred 71
Footbal League 15
Ford 132
Fresh & Easy 69

Gallup Poll 97
Gamble, James 30
Garland-Compton 88
Gates, Bill 19, 92, 94
Gehry, Frank 47
General Foods 31, 37, 104
George 71
Gerstner, Lou 59, 60
Gibbs SR 88
Giddens, Anthony 111
Gillette 33, 65
GIVe 71
Goldman Sachs 22, 28
Google 90, 124, 127
Google AdSense 126
Google News 129
Gould, Philip 110-11
Grade, Michael 90
Granada TV 88
Green & Black's 21, 72
Green, Paul 88, 89
Green, Sir Philip 71
Greenpeace 113, 114-15
Grey 132

Hanson Trust 69
Harley Davidson 80-2
Harley Owners' Group 81, 82
Harrods 61
Hathaway 98
Hayden, Steve 93
Heath, Edward 99-100
Heineken 48, 49, 50
Heinz Tomato Ketchup 20, 141-2

Index

Hellmann's 88
Henry VIII 52-3, 54, 149
Hitler, Adolf 46
Holbein 52
Hollywood 37
Honda 104
Horrocks, Jane 94
Hovis 92
Howard-Spink, Geoff 50
Hudson, Hugh 45, 49
Huffington Post 128-9, 130
Huffington, Arianna 129

IBM 58-60
Ibuka, Masaru 54
InBev 50
Innocent 21, 145
iPhone 128
iTunes 128
ITV 15, 88-9, 90
Ivory 28, 29, 32

J. Walter Thompson 132, 149, 151
Jean de Florette 50
Jobs, Steve 19, 92, 93
John Lewis 144-5
Johnnie Walker Black Label 41
Johnson & Johnson 32

Kaupthing 107
Kawakami, Genichi 22-3
Kennedy, John F. 36
King, Justin 68
Kingsmill 142-3
Kraft 28, 31, 37, 64
Krogers 61-2

Labour Party 109-10, 111
LBC 89
Lehman Brothers 10, 28
Leighton, Alan 67-8, 70-1

Lever, William, 1st Viscount Leverhulme 85
Lloyds Bank 10
London Weekend Television 88
Love in the Afternoon 47
Lovelock, Terry 49
Lowe, Frank 49, 50, 66
Lowe Howard-Spink 50, 66, 94

M&Ms 35
McCann-Erickson 132
McDonald's 22, 147
McDougalls flour 147
McElroy, Neil 30-1, 35-6, 39, 44, 130-1
MacLaurin, Ian 66
Mad Men 33
Madison Avenue 43, 44
Major, Anya 93
Man with the Golden Arm, The 47
Manchester United 15
Mango 69, 70
Manon des Sources 50
Marks & Spencer 61, 70, 147
Marlboro 44
Mars 35
Marsh, Peter 48
Match of the Day 15

Media Buying Services 88
Medici 52
Metcalf, Julian 79, 80
Microsoft 19, 92, 120
Mini 144
Moore, Dudley 66-8
Morita, Akio 55
Morrison, Ken 68
Morrisons 67, 68
Murdoch, Rupert 14, 15, 28, 90, 116, 117
MySpace 126

National Health Service 101

One Hard Question

Nestlé 37, 64, 103, 132, 146
New York Times 133
News Corporation 126
Newsweek 129
Next 71
Nike 145
Nintendo 149-50
Nixon, Richard Milhous 36
Norman, Archie 67-8, 70-1
Norris, Alexander 30

Obama, Barack 133-4
Ogilvy, David 97-8, 107
Ogilvy & Mather 34, 98, 132
Ohsone, Kozo 55
Oil of Olay 33
Orangina 25
Oreo 28
Orwell, George *1984* 93
Oxfam 113-14
Oxo 94

P&G see Procter & Gamble
Packard, Vance *The Hidden Persuaders* 39-40, 42
Palmolive 31
Pampers 32
Parker, Alan 49
Paulsen, Hank 10
Pepsi 19, 37
Per Una 71
Perrier 25, 27
Peters, Michael 47
PG Tips 88
Piggly Wiggly 61
Player's Navy Cut 45
Polman, Paul 131
Porter, Leslie 66
Premier League 15, 16
Pret A Manger 21-2, 79-80
PricewaterhouseCoopers 59

Pringles 31
Procter & Gamble 30-1, 32-3, 39, 42, 51, 64, 65, 88, 89, 98, 127, 131, 132
Proctor, William 30
Pschitt 25
Publicis 35
Puttnam, David 49

Quant, Mary 40

Reckitt Benckiser 64, 65
Red Cross 113, 114
Reeves, Rosser 33, 34-5, 36, 98 *Reality in Advertising* 35
Richardson-Vicks 32-3
Rolls-Royce 98, 147-8
Ronseal 73
Rose, Sir Stuart 70
Rossiter, Leonard 94
Rowntree 64
Royal Bank of Scotland 10
Rushdie, Salman 34
Rutherford, Andrew 101

Saatchi & Saatchi 45, 100
Saatchi, Charles 45, 49, 100, 102
Saatchi, Maurice 100
Safeway 61, 67, 68
Sainsbury's 62-3, 66, 67, 68, 70 Taste the Difference 72
Sam's Club 62
Saunders, Clarence 61
Scales, Prunella 94
Schweppes 98
Scott, Ridley 92-3
Seinfeld, Jerry 94
Shakespeare 53
Shining, The 47
Silk Cut 45
Simon, Neil *The Prisoner of Second Avenue* 44

Index

Simonds-Goodin, Anthony 48, 49
Sky 14, 15, 16, 90, 116
Smith, Fred 82
SmithKline Beecham 132
Sony 54-6
Stain Devils 28
Starbucks 127
Stella Artois 50
Strepsils 65
Swatch 16, 17

TalkTalk 78
Ted Bates agency 33, 35
Terry's 64
Tesco 62-3, 64, 66-8, 69 Finest 72
Thames TV 88
Thatcher, Margaret 97, 99, 100, 102
Thomas, Brent 93
Thomson, Roy, 1st Baron Thomson of Fleet 89
Times, The 28-9
Tobler 64
Toblerone 48
Top Shop 70
Toyota104 Prius 104
Treets 35
Trophy 48
Tu 71
Tweetmeme 147
Twitter 126
Tylenol 147

Unilever 21, 31, 37, 64, 65, 88, 89, 127, 131, 132
Virgin Media 90
Volkswagen Beetle 46

Waitrose 120-1 Essentials 120
Walkman 54-6
Wal-Mart 62, 68, 70
Walsh, Martyn 101

Walton, Sam 62
Weldon, Fay 34
Wella 33
Whitbread 48
Wii 149
Wilkinson Sword 65
Woolworth 48, 61, 68
WPP Group 98, 133
Wray, Edward 24
Wright, Frank Lloyd 47

Yamaha, Torakusu 22
Yamaha 22-3

YouTube 127

Zara 69, 70

157

CPSIA information can be obtained at www.ICGtesting.com
Printed in the USA
BVOW08s0030110215

387247BV00018B/183/P